Happy Cooking!

Edward

FOOD FOR FRIENDS

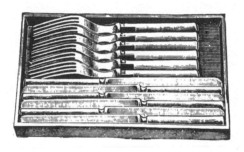

EDWARD HAYDEN

THE O'BRIEN PRESS
DUBLIN

EDWARD HAYDEN is best known for his very popular regular cookery slots on TV3's *Ireland AM*. Edward is the regular cookery columnist in Ireland's leading women's weekly, *Woman's Way*, and his recipes and cookery features have appeared in numerous national publications, including the *Irish Independent*, *The Irish Times*, the *Sunday World* and *Food & Wine Magazine*.

Edward works as a culinary lecturer in Waterford Institute of Technology and regularly guest lectures in An Grianán, the Irish Countrywomen's Association Adult Education Centre and with Anne Neary of Ryeland House Cookery School.

In 2008 Edward self-published his first cookery book, *Edward Entertains* and in 2011 he published *Food to Love* with The O'Brien Press. *Food to Love* quickly became a top-five Irish bestseller, before being awarded the prestigious Kerry Food Book of the Year Award.

Edward's website www.edwardentertains.com, has an up-to-date food blog and is packed with delicious recipes.

DEDICATION

With the deepest of gratitude for her constant worry, prayers and support and for always rowing in behind me in whatever I do, I would like to dedicate this book to my mother, Sally. Although her unyielding support in helping me achieve my career goals in her unique, quiet and gentle way can never be fully repaid, it is greatly appreciated.

ACKNOWLEDGEMENTS

Writing this book has been a very interesting journey and I have greatly enjoyed testing the recipes, cooking the dishes, sharing my family anecdotes and styling the photographs.

Many people have helped me along different legs of this journey and their hard work, interest and dedication to the project has made *Food For Friends* a book that I'm sure will become a staple point of reference and inspiration in your home.

My life between work, cookery demonstrations and recipe-testing is a busy and varied one and the one person who is always there to help with all aspects of it is my mother, Sally; yet again, in preparation for this publication, she has left no stone unturned. Sometimes I just write a shopping list and the groceries magically appear, sometimes I have to rush off and leave a sink full of dirty dishes and on my return they have vanished and sometimes I just crave a cup of tea and it arrives.

I'd like to thank my family and friends for their help in the many and varied tasks they can be given when they call to visit. Thanks also to my niece, Marie, who shared her birthday celebrations with us for the party chapter of the book – although I secretly think she didn't mind!

Carol Marks of Carol Marks Photography was available once again to work on the photography for the book. Her photographs in previous publications have been so well-commended that it's been my privilege, yet again, to work with her. Her patience is amazing and she works tirelessly with me to achieve perfection.

My very good friend, Olivia O' Driscoll, has 'hit the road' with me in recent times helping out on my cookery demonstrations and recipe trials. She always appears to be one step ahead of me and when I need a whisk she will have it in her hand for me! We have, in the past two years, travelled together around Ireland doing cookery demonstrations and we've yet to run out of conversation.

I would like to pay special tribute to the team at The O'Brien Press. They really are a wonderfully-talented group of people. To Michael O' Brien, Mary Webb and Ivan O'Brien, who again invited me to do another book, to my wonderful and eagle-eyed editor Helen Carr, the innovative designer Emma Byrne and to Ruth Heneghan, Clare Kelly and all the team, I would like to express my deepest thanks for turning my thoughts, words and actions into this wonderful publication.

And finally to all my friends who never 'appear' to tire of hearing or advising about the latest chapter in my culinary life – thanks for listening!

CONTENTS

Introduction	page 7
Brilliant Brunches	**9**
Brunch-Style Burger	10
Mixed Grill Skewers	13
Kedgeree	14
Eggs Benedict	15
Edward's Multiseed Brown Bread	17
Edward's Tortilla Española with Chorizo	18
Muffuletta	21
Home-Baking Essentials	**23**
Spiced Hot Cross Buns with Orange & Cinnamon Glaze	24
Lemon & Almond Cake	27
Iced Cupcakes	28
Chocolate Marble Cake	31
Edward's Chocolate Éclairs	32
Sugar-Crusted Cherry Scones	35
Chocolate Chip Cookies	36
Lemon Drizzle Slices	39
Glazed Fruit Tart	40
Children's Birthday Party	**43**
Sweet & Sticky Chicken Drumsticks	44
Sesame Chicken Goujons	47
Spaghetti Bolognaise	48
Penne Pasta with Chunky Sausages & Tomato Cream Sauce	49
Birthday Cake	51
Sizzling Summer Barbecues	**53**
Lemon & Ginger Fish Parcels	54
Garlic & Rosemary-Scented Steaks	57
Spiced Lamb Koftas with Yoghurt Dressing	58
Chargrilled Vegetable Bruschetta with Basil Mayonnaise	59
Seafood Skewers	60
Whole Roasted Sea Bass Stuffed With Lemongrass Chilli	63
Chicken Breasts With Chilli Yoghurt Marinade	64
Summer Salads	**67**
Sweet Chilli Noodle Salad	68
Penne Pasta with Poached Salmon, Roasted Fennel & Lemon Mayonnaise	71
Moroccan Couscous	72
Potato Salad with Pesto, Pine Nuts & Smoked Bacon	75
Salad Selections & Combinations	76
Delicious Dressings	79
Informal Suppers	**81**
Crispy Pork Salad With Cashew Nuts & Sweet Potato Crisps	82
Spiced Indian Pakoras	84
Hungarian Beef Goulash	85
Spaghetti with Sweet Chilli Prawns	87
Beef & Vegetable Noodle Stir Fry	88
Pork & Cider Stroganoff	90
Braised Chicken with Smoked Bacon Cream	91
Whole Roasted Chicken, Lemon, Courgette & Pine Nut Stuffing	92
Italian Baked Chicken	95
Spiced Chickpea Broth	96
Roasted Carrot & Ginger Soup	99
Smoked Haddock Chowder	100
Garlic & Rosemary-Smeared Lamb Cutlets with Garlic Sautéd Potatoes	103

Food For Romance	**105**
Guacamole with Home-Baked Spiced Tortilla Crisps	106
Salad of Roasted Figs, Gorgonzola Cheese & Parma Ham	107
Beef Stroganoff	108
Tandoori Salmon, Spicy Mango & Cucumber Salsa	109
Chocolate & Hazelnut Terrine	110
Movie Night In	**113**
Spicy Chicken Quesadillas	114
Crispy Beef Spring Rolls	115
Crisper Than Crisp Potato Wedges	117
Pitta Pizzas	118
Quiche in a Tin	121
Plotting & Planning a Dinner Party	**123**
White Soda Scones with Cheese & Thyme	124
Creamy Potato, Leek and Thyme Soup	127
Crock of Mussels in White Wine & Cream Broth	128
Spaghetti with Crab Meat And Chilli	129
Crusted Hake with Crunchy Pine Nut Topping	130
Fillet of Beef with Sautéd Spinach and Mushroom with Black Pepper Cream	133
Pork Steak Stuffed with Curried Rice	134
Baked Lemon Sole with Salsa Verde	137
Baked Ginger Pudding, Cinnamon-Roasted Pears & Butterscotch Sauce	138
Chocolate Truffle Cake	141
Edward's Apple & Rhubarb Crumble Cake	142
All the Big Occasions	**145**
Pesto & Sundried Tomato Bread	146
Spiced Winter Vegetable Soup	148
Mediterranean Vegetable Stack	149
Pork & Chicken Terrine	151
Little Pots Of Paté	152
New-Style Coronation Chicken	154
Roast Sirloin of Beef, Traditional Gravy	155
Asian Crusted Salmon	157
Hot & Spicy Beef Curry	158
Rich Lamb Casserole with Gratin Topping	161
Steamed Chocolate Pudding	162
Edward's Special Raspberry Meringue Cake	165
Best-Ever Tiramisu	166
Here Comes Santa Claus	**169**
Edward's Christmas Canapés (five ways to nibble through Christmas)	170
Traditional Roast Turkey Breast with Cranberry Gravy	176
Apple, Cranberry and Sausage-Meat Stuffing	177
Whole Roast Duck With Apricot & Hazelnut Stuffing	178
Vegetarian Moussaka	179
Dundee Cake	180
White Chocolate & Raspberry Trifle	183
Traditional Mincemeat	184
Festive Mince Pie Crumbles	187
Chocolate & Hazelnut Biscotti	188
Index	**190**

First published 2013 by
The O'Brien Press Ltd,
12 Terenure Road East, Rathgar,
Dublin 6, Ireland.
Tel: +353 1 4923333; Fax: +353 1 4922777
E-mail: books@obrien.ie.
Website: www.obrien.ie

Text & Photography © Edward Hayden, 2013
Food Stylist: Edward Hayden, 2013
Photographer: Carol Marks, 2013
Copyright for typesetting, layout, editing, design
© The O'Brien Press Ltd

ISBN: 978-1-84717-364-5

British Library Cataloguing-in-Publication Data
A catalogue record for this title is available from the British Library

1 2 3 4 5 6 7 8
13 14 15 16 17

Printed and bound in Poland by Białostockie Zakłady Graficzne S.A.
The paper in this book is produced using pulp from managed forests

INTRODUCTION

Growing up, our family, like so many Irish families, marked all celebrations with a feast of some sort. My mother baked every day so our house was rarely without either fresh bread or cakes and both my parents instilled in us the sense of occasion and that all occasions should be marked and celebrated.

Reminiscing on this in recent times I thought that this would be a wonderful idea for a cookery book, to dedicate a chapter to all the special occasions that family and friends enjoy together and give them some easy-to-follow recipes and tips specific to the occasion. And so *Food for Friends* began its journey.

I like to think that the occasions I've chosen will be very popular and topical to your own culinary needs. Within each chapter there is a series of specially-chosen recipes, which I feel will very much suit the occasion in question and help you to prepare for those important events for your family and friends.

It is lovely to cook a meal for yourself, but I always think that there's something very satisfying about putting some ingredients together and spending some time cooking up a delicious meal for others to enjoy. As you cook your way through the recipes in the book I'm sure your family and friends will be more than willing to become your chief tasters and will gratefully enjoy all of your culinary endeavours!

I like to think that my style of cooking is straightforward, wholesome home cooking. This is a practical cookery book with easy-to-follow recipes that will hopefully afford you not only a delicious and enjoyable meal, but also the opportunity to spend valuable time with your family and friends without excessive labouring in the kitchen.

Wishing you many happy hours of cooking as you work your way through *Food For Friends*!

Enjoy!

Edward

BRILLIANT BRUNCHES

BRUNCH-STYLE BURGER

I adore this recipe for homemade burgers. If you've skipped breakfast and are looking for a nice early lunch option then I think this is just it!

Serves 6

Burgers:

1¹/₂ lb/700g lean minced beef

1 bunch spring onions/ medium onion, finely sliced

2 tablespoons sweet chilli jam/ tomato ketchup

2 tablespoons parsley, freshly chopped

Salt and freshly-ground black pepper

2oz/50g breadcrumbs

2oz/50g grated cheese (parmesan, cheddar, blue, mozzarella)

1 large egg

A litle plain flour for shaping

A little oil

To Serve:

6 bread rolls/burger buns

Mayonnaise, to garnish 6 burgers

Shredded lettuce, to serve

Sliced tomato, to serve

6 rashers bacon

6 eggs

Put the minced beef into a large mixing bowl, then add the finely-sliced onion or spring onion.

Add in the chilli jam or ketchup, the chopped parsley, breadcrumbs and cheese. Season the mixture with a little salt and pepper.

Add in the egg and mash the mixture together with your hands; the egg will act as a binding agent.

Divide the mixture into six pieces and using a little plain flour shape them into burgers about half an inch/1.5cm thick.

Allow to rest in the fridge for at least thirty minutes.

Preheat the oven to 190C/375F/Gas Mark 5. Heat a large ovenproof frying pan with a little oil. Pan fry the burgers for 2–3 minutes on either side and then transfer to the preheated oven to continue cooking for a further 12-14 minutes until cooked through to the centre.

Cut a bread roll/burger bun in half and grill lightly.

Spread some mayonnaise on top of the bun and then garnish with some shredded lettuce and sliced tomato.

Grill or bake the rashers until nice and crispy and then softly fry the eggs

Serve the burger on the bun, topped with the crispy bacon and a soft fried egg.

EDWARD'S HANDY HINTS: This will make six substantial burgers (more if you make them smaller) so you can wrap them up in cling film and freeze some until they are required. You can also use this recipe to make meatballs to serve with tomato enriched spaghetti.

If you wish to make this recipe on the barbecue just brush the burgers with a little oil to prevent them from sticking and barbecue on either side for 4-5 minutes on a preheated barbecue. Alternatively, you can seal the burgers on the barbecue, then transfer them to a baking sheet and put them into the preheated oven for 10-12 minutes until they are fully cooked. Cut one in the centre just to make sure as undercooked mince is a high-risk product.

MIXED GRILL SKEWERS

A meat lover's heaven!! This is my take on the traditional mixed grill that so many Irish people love to enjoy for breakfast or brunch. It's the perfect option to serve if you have visitors staying with you for a weekend and wish to enjoy a leisurely brunch before they depart. It's difficult to give exact amounts for this recipe; the amounts below will make approx six skewers, but it's really up to you how much you add to each skewer; you can cut down or bulk up on the meat as you prefer.

Serves 6

12 cocktail sausages

6 lamb chops, bones removed

6 rashers of bacon

1 sirloin steak, cut into cubes

2 chicken breasts, cut into cubes

6 cherry tomatoes

Marinade:

4 tablespoons oil

2 sprigs rosemary

2 sprigs thyme

Black peppercorns

4 cloves of garlic, finely chopped

Cut each rasher in half lengthways and roll them each piece up into a swiss roll/coil shape.

Arrange the diced meats on to a long metal skewer in what ever order you desire. I normally do it in the following order but it is completely up to you.

Cocktail sausage, lamb, rolled rashers of bacon, steak, chicken, rolled rasher of bacon, sausage and cherry tomato and then repeat until all skewers are made.

Mix all the ingredients for the marinade together and pour over the skewers. Mix the skewers around gently to ensure an even coating on each.

Preheat the oven to 200C/400F/Gas Mark 6. Place the skewers onto a flat baking tray and bake in the preheated oven for 18-20 minutes.

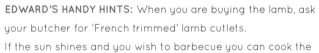

EDWARD'S HANDY HINTS: When you are buying the lamb, ask your butcher for 'French trimmed' lamb cutlets.

If the sun shines and you wish to barbecue you can cook the skewers on the hot barbecue for 10-15 minutes, turning frequently depending on how you like your meat cooked.

Ensure that the chicken and sausages are fully cooked.

KEDGEREE

This is a quintessential English curried rice dish that is served as a breakfast/brunch option. It is reported that the dish became popular in Victorian England after the British colonials returned home from India with the recipe. It's a great warming option to have and it is comfort food at its best. Also if you have over indulged the night before this is the perfect 'pick me up'!

Serves 6

8oz/225g smoked haddock
A little milk, for poaching
2 eggs
2 cloves garlic, diced
1 medium onion, diced
1 small cooking apple, diced
1 green pepper, diced
7oz/200g long-grain rice
1 tablespoon curry powder
14floz/400ml fish stock
Salt & freshly-ground black pepper
1 teaspoon soy sauce, optional
Dash of Worcestershire sauce, optional
1oz/25g sultanas
Parsley, chopped

Begin by poaching the smoked haddock. Place the fish into a shallow saucepan, cover with some milk and bring to the boil. Reduce the heat and simmer gently for 4-5 minutes until it is cooked thoroughly. Remove the fish from the pan, break into large chunks and set aside.

Next, hardboil the eggs by placing in cold, slightly-salted water and bring to the boil. Once the water comes to the boil, boil for 8-9 minutes and then place the saucepan under running cold water until the eggs have cooled down. Peel the eggs, cut them into quarters and set aside.

Heat a shallow-based saucepan and add the diced garlic, onion, apple and green pepper. Cook these over a gentle heat for 3-4 minutes and then add in the rice. Mix thoroughly to ensure the rice is coated and then add in the curry powder. Stir well to allow the powder to infuse the dish.

Pour in the stock, stirring constantly until the mixture comes to the boil. Once the mixture comes to the boil put a tight-fitting lid on the pan, reduce the heat and simmer for 12-15 minutes or until the rice is cooked, stirring occasionally to ensure that the liquid does not evaporate off (add a little extra liquid if required). Once the rice is ready, season lightly with some salt and pepper and some of the soy and Worcestershire sauce. Stir in the sultanas at this stage also along with the cooked smoked haddock.

Transfer the entire mixture to a large serving dish and garnish with the quartered hardboiled eggs and some chopped parsley.

EDWARD'S HANDY HINT: It's fine to use either a mild chicken stock or water if you can't source fish stock.

EGGS BENEDICT

This is a very popular breakfast or brunch dish, which has been given many makeovers and interpretations over the years, but is still a classic and popular dish.

Serves 6

Hollandaise Sauce

3 large egg yolks

1 teaspoon white wine vinegar/ lemon juice

4oz/110g clarified butter (see p 152)

1 tablespoon boiling water (if required)

Salt and freshly-ground black pepper

Eggs Benedict

6 poached eggs

Hollandaise sauce

12 rashers of bacon

6 English muffins/slices toast

Flat-leaf parsley

HOLLANDAISE SAUCE

Heat a large saucepan of water and keep it on a very gentle simmer.

In a separate small saucepan melt the butter and remove it from the heat and use it to make clarified butter (see Edward's Handy Hint p152).

Choose a large spotlessly-clean glass or stainless steel bowl and put the egg yolks into it with the white wine vinegar or lemon juice and whisk well.

Place the bowl over the simmering water and continue to whisk continuously until the egg yolks become light and creamy in colour and consistency. You need to be very careful at this stage because the line between creamy and scrambled is very fine!

Next, add the clarified butter, pouring it in very slowly whilst continuing to whisk – it's a bit of a balancing act at this stage because you will need to take the bowl on and off of the saucepan whilst whisking in the butter but do persevere, the end result is worth it all. It is important to remove the bowl from the water periodically as overheating of the egg mixture can onset scrambling or curdling. If after adding all the butter the sauce is still a little thick for your liking, whisk in the boiling water. Season to taste with a little salt and ground pepper.

POACHED EGGS

Whoever you ask about poaching eggs, they will all give you a slightly different variation or nugget of wisdom, so here is my method below! Though there are many commercial egg poachers and associated devices on the market this is still my preferred method of poaching the humble egg!

Bring a medium saucepan of water to the boil.

Drop in a teaspoon white wine vinegar and remove the saucepan from the heat. I normally swirl the water with a whisk to keep it moving.

Carefully break the eggs (no more than three at a time) into the saucepan and watch as they come together at the bottom of the saucepan.

Return to a very gentle heat and cook for approximately 3-4 minutes until the egg yolks are just firm to the touch.

Drain with a slotted spoon and serve immediately.

ASSEMBLY

Grill the bacon until crispy. Lightly toast the muffin and place onto a serving platter with the bacon on top. Slip the poached eggs onto the bacon and garnish with some hollandaise sauce, cracked black pepper and some flat-leaf parsley.

EDWARD'S MULTISEED BROWN BREAD

Whenever I give cookery demonstrations everyone is always interested in brown bread recipes. I love to have this one at home and I love to enjoy it as a perfect breakfast/brunch option. This bread is delicious toasted also. It has a firm, crusty exterior and a nice, spongy centre which makes it lovely and moist. Sometimes I substitute the mixed seeds for some pine nuts, diced dried apricots or sultanas, which add an unusual finish to this classic bread.

Makes 1 loaf

14oz/400g wholemeal flour

2oz/50g plain flour

2oz/50g porridge oats

Pinch of salt

2 level teaspoons bread soda

2 large eggs

1 tablespoon dark black treacle

Splash of sunflower oil

18floz/500ml buttermilk

3 tablespoons mixed seeds
(pumpkin, sesame, poppy,
sunflower)

Preheat the oven to 170C/325F/Gas Mark 3.

Place the wholemeal flour into a large mixing bowl and sieve in the plain flour and bread soda, then add the salt and porridge oats and mix well.

In a separate bowl beat the eggs together with the oil and dark treacle and add to the dry mixture.

Next mix in the buttermilk and get the mix to a 'sloppy' consistency.

Add two tablespoons of the multiseed mixture to the bread.

Pour into a well greased 2lb/900g loaf tin and smooth the top of the bread with a wet spoon. Sprinkle the remaining seeds on top of the bread and bake in the oven for an hour.

After the hour has elapsed remove the bread from the tin, the top of the bread at this stage will have formed a nice crunchy crust but the sides will still be quite soft so turn the bread upside down, place it back in the tin and return to the oven to bake for a further 20 minutes.

Remove from the oven and allow the bread to cool down.

EDWARD'S HANDY HINTS: This bread stays fresh for about 4-5 days and can be successfully frozen, either whole or sliced.
My neighbour makes this bread, slices it and freezes it in two-slice portions for her convenience.
The mixture can be spooned into well-greased muffin tins to make cute little individual breads and baked for approx 25-30 minutes at 180C/350F/Gas Mark 4.
Fresh milk mixed with lemon juice (1 lemon) or natural yoghurt (3 floz/100ml) can be used in place of buttermilk. Once you have added the juice or the yoghurt just give it a stir and leave it to rest for a few minutes. In total you will still need the same amount of liquid for the recipe.

EDWARD'S TORTILLA ESPAÑOLA WITH CHORIZO

This is a really versatile dish that can be served at any time of day. It's perfect for brunch and I often prepare it with the morning's supply of eggs from the hens. For something with so few ingredients it can be surprisingly tricky to make so give yourself a dry run before serving it up to your mother in law for a special family brunch!

Serves 6

2 tablespoons oil

1 large onion, thinly sliced

4 large potatoes, thinly sliced

3oz/75g chorizo, thinly sliced

5 large eggs

Salt and freshly-ground black pepper

Choose a solid non-stick 9 inch/23 cm pan and gently heat two tablespoons of oil. Dry the sliced onion and potatoes in a cloth and put them into a large mixing bowl. Mix them together and season with a little salt and pepper.

Add the mixture to the pan and toss gently to ensure everything is coated in the oil. Reduce the heat to the lowest setting and cover the pan with a tightly fitting lid or a plate and allow the potatoes and onions to cook, stirring occasionally, for approximately 15-20 minutes.

Meanwhile in a large mixing bowl beat together the eggs with a little seasoning. Check to ensure that the potatoes and onions have softened and then transfer them into the mixing bowl with the eggs and add the thinly-sliced chorizo.

Clean out the frying pan using a clean cloth and return to the heat with the remaining tablespoon oil. Heat gently and then carefully pour in the egg and potato mixture and allow to cook, again on the lowest setting for approximately 15-20 minutes until all of the liquid egg has dried up. Secure a flat plate on top of the pan, carefully invert (turn over) the tortilla onto the plate and then slide it back into the pan to cook the other side for 4-5 minutes.

Remove from the heat and allow to cool in the pan for a further five minutes before inverting onto a serving platter.

Serve either hot or cold with some green salad and chutney.

EDWARD'S HANDY HINTS: Feel free to vary the recipe by adding some frozen peas, sundried tomatoes, bacon lardons or even some cooked chicken.
When the tortilla is cold why not dice it up into bite size portions for a canapé or tapas option.

MUFFULETTA

A muffuletta is a sandwich made and encased in a hollowed out loaf of bread with the top cut off to make the filling. This is an ideal brunch option but is also wonderful for school or work lunchboxes or a summer picnic. You can be as innovative as you like with the filling, using up whatever bits and pieces you have in your fridge.

Serves 6-8

A little oil for cooking

4 tablespoons red onion marmalade (p170)

1 courgette, halved and thinly sliced lengthways

1 red pepper, cut into large chunks

1 yellow pepper, cut into large chunks

1 green pepper, cut into large chunks

1 round loaf of bread (approx 8inch/20cm diameter)

6-8 slices parma ham

6-8 slices salami

12oz/350g brie cheese, sliced

2 tablespoons basil pesto (p75)

Large handful rocket

Preheat the oven to 180C/350F/Gas Mark 4.

Meanwhile place the courgettes and peppers onto a flat roasting tray and drizzle with a little oil.

Allow to cook in the preheated oven for 25-30 minutes until softened and then allow to cool.

Using a sharp knife slice the top off the loaf of bread and set it to one side to act as the lid later on. Scoop the bread out of the centre of the loaf, just leaving a little of the bread attached to the crusts, all the way round.

ASSEMBLY

Spread the base of the bread with the basil pesto mixture, and then arrange three of the slices of parma ham and salami on top of that. Spread this with some red onion marmalade and half of the roasted vegetables. Carefully arrange half the sliced brie and then top with some fresh rocket leaves. Repeat this process with the second half of the ingredients, ensuring that you press down well on the mixture when you add each layer. Once the last layer of rocket has gone in you can place the lid on top.

Wrap the bread in cling film and place onto a flat plate or chopping board. Place another plate on top and weight down with some canned foods to ensure that it will be compact and will cut correctly. Store in the fridge for at least 3-4 hours, but preferably overnight and then unwrap and cut into wedges.

EDWARD'S HANDY HINT: Use the bread which you have scooped out to make some fresh white breadcrumbs for the freezer.

HOME BAKING
ESSENTIALS

SPICED HOT CROSS BUNS WITH ORANGE AND CINNAMON GLAZE

Hot cross buns have been around since around the seventeenth century. They were traditionally baked and eaten on Good Friday – the cross made from flour and water piped on top of the flavoured yeast dough is said to represent the sufferings of Jesus on the cross. Nowadays you can get them throughout the year! I love to give seasonal and edible gifts to my friends; whether it's a Christmas cake for Christmas, chocolate truffles at valentines or these lovely dough buns for Easter I always say 'I'm thinking of you' with some of my sweet temptations!

Serves 12

Batter:

1 x 7g sachet of easy-blend dried yeast

1oz/25g light brown sugar

4oz/110g strong baker's flour

9floz/250ml warm milk

Dough:

10oz/300g strong baker's flour

Pinch salt

1 teaspoon ground cinnamon

$^1/_2$ teaspoon ground nutmeg

Grated zest of 1 orange

2oz/50g butter

2oz/50g brown sugar

7oz/200g sultanas

2 egg yolks mixed with 1 tablespoon water

Cross Ingredients:

2 tablespoons plain flour

A little cold water

Orange & Cinnamon Glaze:

3oz/75g caster sugar

Juice of one orange

1 cinnamon stick

3 floz/100ml water

Preheat to oven to 190C/375F/Gas Mark 5.

Make the batter first by mixing all ingredients together; transfer it to a large bowl (the mixture swells!), cover down some cling film and leave to rise for about half an hour until the mixture has bubbled up and become frothy.

Meanwhile, make the dough. First, sieve the flour, salt, cinnamon and nutmeg together, then add in the orange zest and rub the butter into the dry ingredients. Stir in the sugar and sultanas.

Pour the batter in on top of the dry ingredients and add in the two egg yolks for added richness. Mix until all of the ingredients have come together.

Transfer the mixture onto a floured work surface and knead for 4-5 minutes until the mixture has come together.

Divide the dough into nine balls and place them side by side on a flat baking sheet, leaving a little room between each as they will spread. Cover them with a dry cloth and leave to rise for approximately an hour in a warm environment. When the rolls have risen dramatically (they should have almost doubled in size) blend the flour with some water and pipe a cross on top of each.

Bake in the oven for twenty minutes until golden brown.

ORANGE AND CINNAMON GLAZE

While the buns are baking, make the glaze.

Bring all ingredients to the boil for 3-4 minutes until a thick syrup has been achieved.

Brush the top of the cooked buns with this boiling syrup.

EDWARD'S HANDY HINT: If you run out of time, you can also brush the hot cross buns with boiled apricot jam.

LEMON AND ALMOND CA

This is a fantastic cake and it makes a delicious option to serve a
This Mediterranean-inspired recipe is gluten free also which just

Serves 8

Cake:

6 eggs, separated
7oz/200g sugar
Zest of 2 lemons, grated
10oz/300g ground almonds

Lemon syrup:

5oz/150g sugar
4floz/110ml water
1 lemon, cut into thin slices

Preheat oven to 180C/350F/Gas Mark 4.

Lightly grease an 8 inch/20cm deep round cake tin and line it with baking parchment.

In a mixing bowl beat the egg yolks with the sugar and lemon zest to a pale light cream, add the ground almonds and mix well. At this stage the mixture will be very stiff but don't worry about that!

Stiffly beat the egg whites until they are meringue-like, then beat half of the egg white mixture into the almond mix with a wooden spoon to loosen it up. Gently fold the remaining egg whites into almond mixture with a metal spoon.

Pour into the tin and bake in the pre-heated oven for approximately 40-45 minutes until set. A skewer inserted in the centre should come out clean.

While the cake is baking, make up the lemon syrup.

Put the sugar, sliced lemon and the water into a small saucepan and bring to the boil.

When the cake comes out of the oven immediately pour some of the syrup over the top.

The delicious syrup will soak into the cake as you pour it, making it beautifully moist, so continue to baste or soak the cake regularly until it is all used up.

Decorate the cake with the remaining lemon slices.

ICED CUPCAKES

Cupcakes are really popular now and are so versatile, whether you're having friends over for a stylish get-together or hosting a children's birthday party, they'll go down a treat. I made them recently for a wedding celebration and they were toast of the party!

Makes 12

Cupcakes:

7oz/200g butter, softened

7oz/200g caster sugar

5 large eggs

14oz/400g plain flour

1 rounded teaspoon baking powder

Topping:

6oz/175g butter, softened

12oz/350g icing sugar

$\frac{1}{2}$ teaspoon vanilla extract

1 tablespoon boiling water

Garnish: (optional)

6oz/175g roll-out icing

Food colouring

Preheat the oven to 180C/350F/Gas Mark 4.

Fill a 12-cup muffin tray with muffin papers.

In a large mixing bowl cream the butter and sugar until they are light and fluffy. Add in the eggs.

Add the baking powder to the flour and lightly sieve that into the buttery mixture.

Continue to cream the mixture together lightly until a smooth dropping consistency has been achieved.

Divide the mixture between the muffin cases and pop the tray into the oven for approximately 20-25 minutes or until golden brown.

Allow to cool whilst making the butter-icing topping.

Place the softened butter and icing sugar into a large mixing bowl with the vanilla extract and cream until light and fluffy. Add the boiling water to get an extra smooth and light consistency.

Meanwhile knead a little food colouring into the roll-out icing to colour it. Sometimes I divide it in pieces and dye the icing a variety of colours. Roll out the icing and cut out a series of small hearts from the icing. Leave on a tray lined with parchment and allow to firm up.

Using a piping bag, pipe a large swirl of butter icing onto each cupcake and then top with a coloured heart.

Store in an airtight container until required.

CHOCOLATE MARBLE CAKE

I bake quite a lot at home and this particular recipe is one I often call upon. It's so simple and very tasty. It's a perfect afternoon tea option, or if you are invited round to a friend's house this would be a great dessert to bring with you as a gift.

Serves 8-10

8oz/225g butter

8oz/225g caster sugar

8oz/225g self-raising flour

5 eggs

3oz/75g dark chocolate or 1 tablespoon cocoa powder

Topping:

2oz/50g dark chocolate

2oz/50g white chocolate

Lightly grease and line an 8inch/20cm deep cake tin.

Preheat the oven to 180C/325F/Gas Mark 4.

Cream the butter and sugar together in a mixing bowl until light and fluffy.

Sieve the self-raising flour.

Add in the eggs the sifted flour to the buttery mix and stir until completely combined.

Divide the mixture in half.

Melt the dark chocolate and mix into one half of the mixture. If using cocoa powder instead of the dark chocolate add it at this stage.

Spoon the plain mixture into the tin (leaving space for some dark to go in beside it).

When you have used all of the plain mixture, spoon in the dark chocolate mixture.

Level the mixture roughly with a spoon, then take a sharp knife, put it into the cake mixture and push it back and forward to create a marbled effect.

Transfer the cake to the preheated oven and bake for approximately 40-45 minutes until a skewer inserted in the centre comes out clean.

Allow to cool and then remove from the cake tin and coat the top with some drizzles of melted dark and white chocolate (melted separately).

When the chocolate has set cut the cake into slices and serve.

EDWARD'S CHOCOLATE ÉCLAIRS

People tend to have a fear of choux pastry and so rarely or never make it. It is, in fact, one of the easiest pastries to make providing you follow the very simple rules. Éclairs are a very popular option and if you are visiting family and friends I'm sure a plate of chocolate éclairs would be very gratefully received – and if you serve them to your own guests, they'll be sure to come again!

Makes 12-15

Éclairs:

9 floz/250 ml cold water

4oz/110g butter

Pinch of sugar and salt

5oz/150g strong flour

4 large eggs

Filling:

8 floz/225 ml whipped cream

Ganache topping:

4oz/110g dark chocolate

2 floz/50 ml pouring cream

Preheat the oven to 180C/350F/Gas Mark 4.

Grease two baking sheets with melted butter.

Put the butter, water, salt & sugar in a large saucepan and bring to the boil. It is important that the mixture comes to the boil; if you just melt it and do not allow it to come to the boil the mixture will go dramatically wrong. Take the saucepan off the heat.

Sift the flour and add it, all at once, to the boiling liquid.

Stir rapidly with a wooden spoon.

Return the saucepan to the heat and beat continuously until the mixture comes clean away from the sides of the saucepan. You are cooking the flour at this stage. Transfer to a large mixing bowl and allow to cool for about five minutes.

In a separate bowl whisk the eggs together, then slowly beat them into the cooked paste. I use an electric whisk as the mixture can be quite stiff. Add the eggs little by little, beating thoroughly between each addition.

Using a piping bag, pipe the choux pastry into long strips about 4 inches/10cm long. You should get approximately 12-15 éclairs out of the mix. Bake for 30-35 minutes; they should sound hollow when tapped underneath.

Remove from the oven and allow them to cool on a wire rack.

Meanwhile make the icing. Place the cream into a medium saucepan and heat gently. Chop the chocolate into pieces and whisk it into the warmed cream and continue to whisk over a low heat until a smooth, glossy icing is achieved.

When they are cool, split each éclair, fill with the whipped cream and spread with the dark chocolate ganache topping.

SUGAR-CRUSTED CHERRY SCONES

There is something so satisfying about a homemade scone. I love to have a batch on stand-by in the freezer for unexpected callers. I think the crust on these scones makes for very pleasant consumption!

Makes 10-12

1lb/450g plain flour

1 level teaspoon baking powder

4oz/110g caster sugar

Pinch of salt

2oz/50g butter, cold

4oz/110g cherries, chopped

1 egg

5floz/150ml milk, approx

To Garnish:

Egg wash (1 egg mixed with 2 tablespoons milk)

1oz/25g granulated sugar

A little icing sugar, for dusting

Preheat the oven to 190C/375F/Gas Mark 5.

Sieve the flour and baking powder together into a large bowl.

Add the salt and caster sugar to the mix.

Rub in the butter with your fingertips, then add the chopped cherries.

In a separate bowl beat the egg and add to the dry ingredients.

Gradually add the milk at this stage and mix together to a soft dough.

If the mixture is too wet & loose at this stage add in a little extra flour.

Transfer the mixture to a floured surface and flatten it out to about 1 inch/2 ½ cm in depth. Using a scone cutter or a glass, cut out some shapes and transfer to a lined baking tray.

Make up a little egg wash by mixing 1 egg with some milk and brush this over the top of the scone.

Sprinkle with a little granulated sugar and bake for 17-20 minutes, until they are risen and golden brown in colour.

Remove from the oven and dust with icing sugar.

Serve with homemade jam and freshly-whipped cream.

EDWARD'S HANDY HINTS: If you wish to make fruit scones you need to soak 3oz/75g sultanas in a little orange juice or whiskey for half an hour and add these to the mixture just before you add the egg and milk.

If you would like a richer and more indulgent scone, substitute a little cream for some of the milk.

Be aware that – depending on how much you have handled the dry ingredients and how exact you have been with your measurements – you may need a little extra milk or cream to bring the mixture together.

CHOCOLATE CHIP COOKIES

Chocolate chip cookies are a great option to have at home. I have a large glass jar beside the kettle and I fill it with all sorts of sweet treats to have with an afternoon caffeine fix. One of my favourites are these chocolate chip cookies – when they are in the jar they get a quick dispatch. Also if I'm having an impromptu dinner party they are a great dessert option to serve with ice cream and oodles of dark chocolate sauce.

Makes 12-15

3oz/75g butter, softened
3oz/75g light brown sugar
$\frac{1}{2}$ teaspoon vanilla extract
2 eggs
7oz/200g plain flour
$\frac{1}{2}$ teaspoon baking powder
Pinch salt
2oz/50g mixed chocolate chips
2oz/50g mixed nuts, such as
pistachios, walnuts, shelled
hazelnuts and pine nuts

Preheat the oven to 180°C/350°F/Gas mark 4.

Cream the butter and sugar with the vanilla extract for 4–5 minutes in a large mixing bowl until light and fluffy.

Add the eggs and beat for a few minutes.

Sift the flour with the baking powder and the salt. Measure out the mixed nuts and the chocolate chips.

Add the sifted flour mixture to the butter and egg mixture and beat slowly until the mixture comes together. Next, add the chocolate chips and mixed nuts and beat until combined.

Break some of the dough into small balls and place on a lined baking tray.

Bake for 12–15 minutes in the oven.

Allow to cool down and serve.

EDWARD'S HANDY HINTS: This mixture freezes quite successfully: to freeze it, roll it into long thick coils and then you can cut the mixture more easily.

The cookies will still be quite soft when they come out of the oven, so if you wish you can stick a lollipop stick into the centre to make quirky chocolate-chip lollipops!

LEMON DRIZZLE SLICES

At home when we were young we had the 'bun press'; when visitors
seemed to supply. These tangy lemon slices are for all your unexpected

Makes 10-12 slices

8oz/225g butter, softened
8oz/225g caster sugar
Zest of 1 lemon
4 eggs
1 tablespoon milk
8oz/225g self-raising flour
1 teaspoon baking powder

Topping:
4oz/110g icing sugar
Zest & juice of 1 lemon

Preheat the oven to 180C/350F/Gas Mark 4.

Grease and line an 11 x 7 inch/28cm x 18cm brownie/traybake tray with parchment paper.

Place the butter, sugar and lemon zest into the electric mixer and beat for 3-4 minutes until it has a pale, creamy consistency. Whisk in the eggs and milk and then sift in the flour and baking powder and beat for another 2-3 minutes.

Transfer into the prepared cake tin and bake in the oven for 40-45 minutes or until a skewer inserted in the centre comes out clean.

Allow to cool on a wire rack.

Meanwhile make up the topping.

Mix the lemon juice and most of the zest with the icing sugar and beat until a runny consistency has been achieved. Extra lemon juice or boiling water can be used to loosen further if required.

Drizzle or spread the icing over the top of the cake and then cut the cake into 10-12 slices and garnish with some leftover lemon zest.

EDWARD'S HANDY HINT: I normally cut all the crusts off before I cut into slices; you can decide yourself what to do with the crusts!

GLAZED FRUIT TART

Although this particular recipe has several different stages and takes a bit of time to make, it is definitely well worth the effort. Perfecting this recipe gives you the chance to evoke a Parisian patisserie in your own home and allows your family and friends to enjoy the fruits of your labour.

Serves 8

Biscuit Pastry

4oz/110g butter

4oz/110g caster sugar

1 egg

9oz/250g plain flour

Pastry Cream:

$\frac{1}{2}$ vanilla pod

10 floz/300ml milk

2oz/50g caster sugar

3 egg yolks

1 tablespoon flour

Garnish:

2 tablespoons apricot jam

2 tablespoons water

Selection of fresh fruit (kiwi, peaches, strawberries, grapes, apples, pears, blackberries)

BISCUIT PASTRY

Place the flour, butter, caster sugar and egg into an electric beater and mix for a couple of minutes until the pastry comes together. Wrap in cling film and allow to rest.

After at least an hour in the fridge, roll the pastry out on a floured work surface and use it to line a greased 8inch/20cm loose-bottomed flan ring.

Blind bake the tart (See Edward's Handy Hints).

PASTRY CREAM

Using a sharp knife scrape the seeds from the vanilla pod. Place the vanilla pod and seeds into a large saucepan with the milk and bring the milk to the boil.

Mix the caster sugar and egg yolks together and whisk until pale and creamy.

Add in the flour and mix to a smooth paste.

Pour the boiled milk onto the mixture and return the mixture to a clean pan

Return to a very low heat and cook the mixture thoroughly, stirring constantly, until the mixture has thickened.

Place in a clean bowl and allow to cool down completely.

Cover and store in the fridge until required.

ASSEMBLY

Place the apricot jam into a small saucepan with the water and bring to the boil.

Carefully slide the blind-baked pastry case onto a large serving platter or cake stand, then fill it with the pastry cream.

Neatly arrange some fresh fruit on top and then brush with boiled apricot jam

Allow to set and then serve.

EDWARD'S HANDY HINT: To bake blind: line the tartlet mould with a layer of parchment paper; fill with uncooked rice/dried lentil or chickpeas. Place this in the oven (180C/350F/Gas Mark 4) for 15 minutes and then remove the rice etc and the paper and bake for a further 8 minutes. This leaves you with a perfect tartlet shell and the sides will not fall in. If you wish you could brush the pastry with a little egg white before re-baking to harden up the pastry and prevent it from becoming soggy later on.

CHILDREN'S BIRTHDAY PARTY

SWEET AND STICKY CHICKEN DRUMSTICKS

These are perfect for a children's birthday party. They are messy and delicious in equal measure – what's not to love about that? Just mind the sticky little hands afterwards and watch where they go!! This recipe is very handy for a party as you can make the marinade the night before, leave the chicken in it overnight and then just bake for the party.

Makes 12

12 chicken drumsticks

3 tablespoons soy sauce

1 tablespoon honey

1 teaspoon wholegrain mustard

Dash Worcestershire sauce

2 tablespoons water

2 sprigs thyme

Garnish:

Sesame seeds

Preheat the oven to 180C/350F/Gas Mark 4.

In a large bowl, mix the soy sauce, honey, wholegrain mustard, Worcestershire sauce and thyme. Then whisk in the water, add the chicken drumsticks and allow them to marinate for a couple of hours, or preferably overnight if time allows.

Line a deep roasting tray or dish with a double layer of parchment paper (you will be glad you did this later on!). Pour the chicken drumsticks and the marinade on to the tray, ensuring that the chicken drumsticks are spaced out. Cover the tray tightly with a double layer of tinfoil and place in the oven for an hour.

After the hour, remove the tinfoil and return the tray to the oven for a further 5-10 minutes to crisp up the drumsticks.

Once the drumsticks are fully cooked, remove from the oven, sprinkle with sesame seeds and serve!

SESAME CHICKEN GOUJONS

These are a great and tasty alternative to shop-bought chicken nuggets; your children will love them. It is one of those dishes that children love to help with, so perhaps they could help with the coating of the chicken strips, before they are deep fried by the adults.

Makes 16-20 goujons

4 chicken fillets
1 egg & 2floz /50ml milk
2oz/50g seasoned flour (plain flour with salt and pepper)
5oz/150g breadcrumbs
1 tablespoon sesame seeds

Begin by cutting the chicken fillets into four or five thin strips. Then prepare the ingredients for coating the goujons: put the seasoned flour in one bowl, the beaten egg and milk in another and the breadcrumbs mixed with sesame seeds in another. Dip the pieces of chicken in the flour first to coat, shake off the excess and then transfer to the egg mixture, coating completely, and finally toss the egg-coated pieces of chicken in the breadcrumb mixture. Using your hands, gently press the breadcrumbs onto the pieces of chicken.

TO COOK

Preheat the oven to 180C/350F/Gas Mark 4. Line a baking tray with baking parchment. Heat the deep fat fryer to the recommended level with some vegetable or sunflower oil. Check that the oil is hot enough by dropping cubes of white bread into the oil for thirty seconds – if the bread turns golden brown and crispy in that time, the oil is hot enough. Carefully drop the coated chicken goujons (in batches of approximately 6 or 8 goujons) into the deep fat fryer. Deep fry the chicken until golden brown. This should take no more than 2–3 minutes. Transfer to the prepared baking tray and finish cooking them in the oven for a further 12-15 minutes or until cooked through. Ensure that the chicken is cooked by cutting into the thickest piece with a sharp knife – no pink at all should remain. Serve with some peas and tomato ketchup and perhaps some crisper than crisp potato wedges (p117).

EDWARD'S HANDY HINTS: If sesame seeds are not to your taste, why not try adding approximately 3oz/75g grated parmesan or white cheddar?

If you don't have a deep fat fryer you can shallow-fry the chicken goujons in a deep sauté pan.

The same approach of coating in seasoned flour, egg wash and breadcrumbs can be used for fish, mushrooms or chunks of soft cheese.

SPAGHETTI BOLOGNAISE

Regardless of when it is served, spaghetti bolognaise is a very popular dish, but it's especially popular with children so if and when I'm set the important challenge of catering my niece's birthday party this is one of my favourite dishes to cook. I know the children will enjoy it, as will the adults!

Serves 6-8

A little oil for cooking
1 medium onion, finely chopped
4 cloves garlic, peeled and
crushed
4oz/110g bacon lardons
1 carrot, diced
8 mushrooms, thinly sliced
2lb/900g beef mince
$\frac{1}{2}$ glass red wine (optional)
2 x 14oz/400g tins chopped
tomatoes
2floz/50ml cream
$\frac{1}{2}$ teaspoon dried mixed herbs
Salt and freshly-ground black
pepper

To Serve:
10oz/300g spaghetti
Parmesan cheese, grated

Heat the oil in a large, wide-based frying pan and sauté the onion and garlic with the bacon lardons, carrots and mushrooms for 3-4 minutes, until they are beginning to soften.

Add the mince and mix thoroughly, allowing the beef to seal off; continue cooking until all the meat has browned.

Add the red wine (if using) and allow the mixture to cook gently.

Next add the chopped tomatoes, the cream and the mixed herbs and allow the mixture to come to the boil. Reduce the heat at this stage and continue cooking on a low heat, stirring occasionally for approximately 25-30 minutes until the majority of the liquid has reduced. Season with salt and freshly-ground black pepper to taste.

Cook the spaghetti according to the packet instructions and serve with the bolognaise sauce and lots of grated parmesan cheese.

PENNE PASTA WITH CHUNKY SAUSAGES AND TOMATO CREAM SAUCE

Here I have teamed two foods that always seem to be popular with children – pasta and sausages. If your children don't like these perennial favourites, feel free to adapt the recipe to their tastes by substituting chicken for the sausages and using onions or peppers instead of the mushrooms.

Serves 6-8

A little oil, for cooking
8oz/225g penne pasta
6 large butchers' sausages
2 cloves garlic, crushed
6-8 medium-sized mushrooms, sliced
14oz/400g tinned chopped tomatoes
3floz/75ml cream

To Serve:
Parmesan cheese (optional)
Fresh rocket

Bring a large saucepan of water to the boil and cook the pasta according to the packet instructions.

While the pasta is cooking, cut each sausage into three pieces. Choose a large, wide-based sauté pan, heat a little oil, add the sausages and cook on a medium heat until they are browned all over. Next add the garlic and mushrooms and continue to cook for 2-3 minutes, until they begin to soften.

Pour in the chopped tomatoes and cream and allow the mixture to come to the boil, reduce the heat and simmer for 4-5 minutes. Drain the pasta and add it into the tomato-based sauce and mix well.

Serve immediately in large bowls with some grated parmesan cheese and a little fresh rocket.

BIRTHDAY CAKE

Have you ever wanted to make a delicious birthday, or celebration cake for that special family occasion? This is the recipe for you. A delicious sponge filled with fresh fruit and cream, covered in cream and decorated with some chocolate writing – ready to be devoured by all the party-goers!

Serves 10-12

Sponge:

6 large eggs
6oz/175g caster sugar
6oz/175g self-raising flour

Garnish:

2 tablespoons raspberry jam
Fresh fruit (strawberries, raspberries, blueberries, kiwi and mandarin)
Approximately 1 pint/600ml whipped cream
Melted chocolate to write/ decorate
A little cocoa for dusting

Preheat the oven to 180C/350F/Gas Mark 4.

Grease a 9 inch/23 cm springform tin with melted butter and line with parchment paper.

Whisk the eggs and the sugar together in a large mixing bowl for 4-5 minutes or until the mixture is very well volumised and holds the 'figure of 8' when written with the whisk.

Sieve the flour. Gently fold in sieved flour, being careful not to over-mix and knock the air out of the mixture.

Pour the mixture into the prepared tin and bake for 25-30 minutes. When cooked, the mixture should be springy and coming away from the side of the tin. Allow to cool on a wire rack.

To assemble, split the sponge in two, with a sharp knife, place one piece onto a large serving platter and spread with raspberry jam. Next spread with a little of the freshly-whipped cream and finally a selection of fresh fruit.

Place the remaining piece of sponge on top and press down gently to ensure an even surface. Cover the entire cake with cream and, using a piping bag, pipe some additional cream around the top and bottom and garnish as desired with a selection of fresh fruit.

Melt the chocolate and using a small piping bag write a special message on the top of the cake. Dust lightly with cocoa.

Watch it disappear!

SIZZLING
SUMMER
BARBECUES

LEMON AND GINGER FISH PARCELS

This is a favourite of mine; it works very well as a quick meal for all the family and can be prepared whilst waiting for the barbecue to heat up. 'En Papilotte' is a French culinary term, which means 'paper bag cookery' – this denotes the way this fish is cooked in a vacuum of steam.

Serves 6

1½ mixed peppers (½ each of green, red, yellow)

1 medium carrot

1 red onion

4oz/110g mange-tout/green beans

1 inch root ginger, chopped finely

6 salmon darnes (5oz/150g) each

1 lemon, thinly sliced

Salt & freshly-ground black pepper

6 parsley sprigs

1oz/25g butter (optional)

Cut out six sheets of parchment paper, each approximately A4 sized, then cut out six slightly larger pieces of tinfoil.

Place a piece of parchment paper on top of each piece of tinfoil on a flat work surface.

Thinly slice the vegetables into evenly-sized pieces and mix together in a bowl.

Neatly arrange a portion of the vegetables on top of each piece of baking parchment, then sprinkle with some chopped ginger.

Gently place a salmon darne on top of each vegetable portion, season the fish with a little salt and freshly-ground black pepper and garnish with a slice of lemon and some parsley. Add a little butter also if you wish.

Fold the parchment paper over from each side and twist either end, making sure that all the fish is covered and sealed in. Do not have too much paper wrapped around the fish as this will increase the cooking time.

Fold the tinfoil into a looser package around the parchment-wrapped fish.

Place on the barbecue and cook, closing the lid of the barbecue to create an oven effect, for twenty minutes.

Serve immediately in the little paper parcel. Allow your guests to open their own parcel and be met with the wonderful cooking aromas of the fragrant fish parcel. Serve with a large salad and some crusty bread.

EDWARD'S HANDY HINTS: If it rains, bake the parcels, without the layer of tin foil, in the oven at 190C/375F/Gas Mark 5 for twenty minutes.
Other suitable fish: haddock, monkfish, pollock, cod or similar. You can use a variety of vegetables in these parcels, so vary it as much as you like.

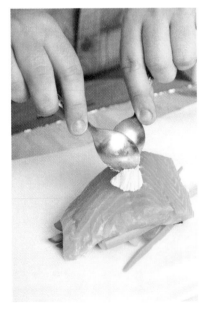

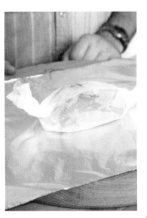

GARLIC AND ROSEMARY-SCENTED STEAKS

I like to use a mild marinade as anything over-flavoured will take from the flavour of the meat, so this recipe is super simple.

Serves 6

3 strip loin steaks (8oz/225g each)
3-4 stems of rosemary, roughly chopped
6 cloves garlic, finely chopped
5-6 black peppercorns, crushed
3 tablespoons oil
1 tablespoon balsamic vinegar (optional)

Lay the steaks out flat in a large dish.

Mix together the chopped garlic, rosemary and crushed peppercorns. Add in the oil and the balsamic vinegar and mix well. Pour this over the steaks and leave to marinate, preferably overnight, but for at least a couple of hours to allow the flavours to develop. Because this is a mild marinade you can leave it for up to 2-3 days.

Heat the barbecue to maximum and cook as follows:

Rare: 2 minutes on either side

Medium: 4 minutes on either side

Well done: 5 minutes on either side

Serve the steaks with some salads (p76) some grilled tomatoes and some garlic butter (p103).

EDWARD'S HANDY HINTS: Try not to over-agitate the meat whilst it is on the grill, instead turn it just once.
This is a very simple, versatile marinade; why not consider using it with chicken, lamb or pork?

SPICED LAMB KOFTAS WITH YOGHURT DRESSING

Every summer I host impromptu barbecues at home. I love nothing more than dusting down the barbecue, whipping up some simple salads, chilling the wine and texting a few friends to call by. When they do, I often cook up these delicious lamb koftas as a nice alternative to the traditional burger.

Serves 6

1 ¹/₂ lb/700g minced lamb
2oz/50g breadcrumbs
¹/₂ teaspoon of ground coriander
1 teaspoon of ground cumin
1 red onion, chopped
2 cloves of garlic, crushed
1 egg
2 tablespoons natural yoghurt
1 tablespoon mint, chopped

Yoghurt Dressing:

7floz/200ml natural yoghurt
1 tablespoon mint, finely chopped
2 cloves garlic, finely chopped

Select 6-8 metal barbecue skewers.

Mix all ingredients for the koftas together in a bowl until thoroughly combined. Divide the mixture into 6-8 pieces, roll into long cylindrical shapes and thread them onto your desired skewers.

COOKING INSTRUCTIONS

Preheat the barbecue. Brush the koftas with oil and cook for approximately 4-5 minutes each side on the barbecue to get a chargrilled effect. Transfer then to a cooler part of the barbecue for a further 6-8 minutes to continue cooking. Alternatively, if it's not barbeque weather, preheat the oven to 190C/375F/Gas Mark 5): place the koftas in the oven for 18-20 minutes until they are cooked through.

Make sure they are fully cooked through to the centre before serving. When cooked they will be firm to the touch, but if you are unsure you could cut one in the centre to check.

YOGHURT DRESSING

Mix all the ingredients together, chill and serve.

EDWARD'S HANDY HINTS: Make the koftas in advance and re-frigerate them well before cooking; this will prevent them from falling apart.
Feel free to use minced beef instead of the lamb.

CHARGRILLED VEGETABLE BRUSCHETTA WITH BASIL MAYONNAISE

Barbecues, by their nature, tend to be very much geared at the carnivores amongst us. Sometimes vegetarians can be left out when it comes to barbecues, but you can create some really great vegetarian options with a little imagination. This dish also makes a great starter for all the barbecue guests.

Serves 6-8

1 red pepper

1 green pepper

1 yellow pepper

1 courgette

2 red onions

Salt & cracked black pepper

2 thyme sprigs, chopped

3 cloves garlic, finely chopped

2 tablespoons oil

Basil Mayonnaise:

2 tablespoons mayonnaise

1 tablespoon basil pesto

2 cloves garlic, crushed

To Serve:

Toasted baguettes/ciabatta breads

Basil mayonnaise

Flat-leaf parsley

Cut the vegetables into large chunks and slices; try and cut them all at varying angles.

Season with a little salt and cracked black pepper.

Break the thyme sprigs into the vegetables and add the chopped garlic.

Drizzle with the oil and mix well.

COOKING INSTRUCTIONS

Preheat the barbecue and grill the vegetables in batches, for 2-3 minutes on either side, transferring them to a warm place when they are cooked through. Mix them together in a large bowl.

If it's not barbecue weather, preheat the oven to 190C/375F/Gas Mark 5. Place all the vegetables on a flat baking tray and cook in the preheated oven for 20-25 minutes. Allow to cool down.

BASIL MAYONNAISE

Just mix all the ingredients together in a bowl.

ASSEMBLY

Spread the toasted bread with some of the basil mayonnaise and then pile high with the chargrilled vegetables. Drizzle, if desired, with some additional basil mayonnaise and garnish with a sprig of flat-leaf parsley.

EDWARD'S HANDY HINT: If you wish you can whisk a little milk into the mayonnaise to achieve a consistency more conducive to drizzling.

SEAFOOD SKEWERS

Cooking seafood on a barbecue can be a difficult and precarious task as it tends to break up and get stuck to the barbecue, but with this simple method of threading small pieces on skewers it just works perfectly. Also it is great to be able to experience a variety of different types of seafood and shellfish in each portion. Feel free to vary the types of fish you use!

Serves 6

Seafood Skewers:

2 large darnes salmon (approx 7oz/200g each)

2 portions monkfish (approx 7oz/200g each)

6 scallops

12 large king prawns

6 cherry tomatoes

1 red onion, cut into six chunks

Marinade:

3 tablespoons oil

1 tablespoon fresh herbs (parsley, dill, fennel, chives), finely chopped

1/2 teaspoon chilli flakes, crushed (optional)

Select six suitable barbecue skewers. Cut the salmon into six pieces and then do the same with the monkfish. Thread the fish and vegetables onto the skewers; allocating two pieces of salmon and two pieces of monkfish to each skewer along with one scallop, two prawns, one whole cherry tomato and a chunk of red onion. Arrange the skewers into a large flat baking dish and prepare the marinade. Mix together the oil and herbs, along with the chilli flakes if using and pour this mixture over the seafood skewers and mix around to coat them all in the marinade. Allow them to marinade for at least 20 minutes before cooking.

COOKING INSTRUCTIONS

Preheat the barbecue. Cook the skewers for approximately 2-3 minutes each side on the barbecue and then move to a slightly cooler part of the barbecue, close the lid and continue cooking for a further 6-8 minutes until cooked through. Alternatively, preheat the oven to 190C/375F/Gas Mark 5. Place the baking dish of seafood skewers in the oven for 12-15 minutes until they are cooked through. Serve with some green salad and lime wedges.

EDWARD'S HANDY HINTS: I am not a fan of the wooden skewers for barbecue cookery. They are fine for use in the oven, but regardless of how much you soak them they are still inclined to burn on the barbecue, so I prefer to use the metal ones. If you are only marinating the skewers for a short time feel free to add in some lemon zest or juice or some finely-chopped capers to the marinade.

WHOLE ROASTED SEA BASS STUFFED WITH LEMONGRASS CHILLI

This is a wonderfully fragrant dish and is so easy to prepare.
If you wish, you can make this dish without the head if you feel it won't endear itself to your guests!

Serves 4

4 whole sea bass (not overly large)

2 red chilli

2 stalks of lemongrass

Bunch fresh coriander (couple of stalks in each sprig)

Salt & freshly-ground black pepper

2 limes, cut into slices

A little oil, for drizzling

12 cherry tomatoes, to garnish

Leaving the head and tail intact, clean out the sea bass or have the fishmonger prepare them for you.

Halve the red chillies and insert half a chilli in the middle of each sea bass. Insert half a stalk of lemongrass into the cavity, along with the sprigs of coriander.

COOKING INSTRUCTIONS

Preheat the barbecue. Lay four large pieces of tinfoil onto a flat work surface and place some baking parchment on top of the foil. Brush the parchment generously with oil and then arrange some sliced lime in the middle. Place the stuffed sea bass on top of the limes and then loosely wrap the parchment and foil around each fish. Place the parcels on the barbecue and cook for 18-20 minutes depending on the size of the fish. To serve just open the parcel slightly or better still allow each guest to open their own!

Alternatively, preheat the oven to 190C/375F/Gas Mark 5. Lay the filled sea bass on a baking sheet, drizzle with the lime juice and a little oil and arrange slices of lime around them. Scatter with a little salt and cracked black pepper and place in the oven. Roast the fish for 20-22 minutes depending on the size of the fish. Serve with some cherry tomatoes.

CHICKEN BREASTS WITH CHILLI YOGHURT MARINADE

My barbecue recipes are really quick and simple to prepare because by their very nature barbecues tend to be impromptu – they are dictated and governed by the weather. Chicken is a very popular item to cook on the barbecue, but it sometimes needs a helping hand. This recipe is perfect for cooking on the barbecue or for a varied effect try using the marinade on some diced chicken before stir-frying.

Serves 6

6 chicken breasts
3 tablespoons natural yoghurt
1 teaspoon crushed chilli flakes
Splash of oil
1 tablespoon parsley or
coriander, freshly-chopped
Zest 1 lime
Cracked black pepper

The first thing I do is to split the chicken breasts in two so as to make them easier to cook through on the barbecue. I split them through the centre, making two fillets out of one. Alternatively you could just cover the full chicken breast with a freezer bag or cling film and use a rolling pin to flatten it and make it thinner.
To make the marinade, mix the yoghurt, chilli flakes, oil and chopped parsley or coriander with the lime zest and cracked black pepper.
Place the chicken breasts into a large bowl and pour the marinade over them, mixing thoroughly to ensure that the chicken is fully coated. Allow the chicken to marinate for at least 10-15 minutes or longer (even overnight if time allows). Heat the barbecue and cook the thin chicken breasts for about 4–5 minutes on either side. Cook the chicken with the lid on the barbecue as it creates an oven effect that will cook the chicken without browning.

EDWARD'S HANDY HINT: This chicken is delicious served either hot or cold on some green salad, or stuffed into a pitta bread or tortilla wrap.

SUMMER
SALADS

SWEET CHILLI NOODLE SALAD

This is a great salad, either a healthy lunch option or to accompany some sizzling summer barbecue options. You can play around with this recipe to suit yourself. I think it's great for using up any vegetables you may have in your fridge at the end of the week, so add whatever takes your fancy.

Serves 6

4 'shells' of dried noodles

5-6 mushrooms, sliced

1½ mixed peppers, thinly sliced

3oz/75g mangetout

1 red onion, sliced

½ cucumber, diced

12 cherry tomatoes

4 tablespoons of sweet chilli jam

1 tablespoon natural yoghurt/ mayonnaise

1 tablespoon oil

Juice of 1 lime

½ teaspoon of dried crushed chilli flakes, optional

Salt & freshly-ground black pepper

Spring onions, chopped, for garnish

2oz/50g cashew nuts

Cook the noodles according to the packet instructions. When they are cooked strain them into a sieve and place them under cold running water. Keep the water running until the noodles are completely cold. This process is known as blanching and refreshing. Drain them well and transfer to a large bowl.

Stir-fry the vegetables (mushrooms, peppers, mangetout, onions) for 3-4 minutes until warmed and softened slightly, but still retaining their colour and slightly crisp. Sprinkle with the chilli flakes (if using). Transfer the vegetable mixture to a bowl and allow to cool down completely.

Mix the cooled vegetables into the blanched and refreshed noodles. Stir in the cucumber and cherry tomatoes together with the chilli jam, yoghurt/mayonnaise, oil, and lime juice. Season.

Arrange salad in a large bowl and scatter with chopped spring onions and cashew nuts.

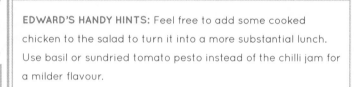

EDWARD'S HANDY HINTS: Feel free to add some cooked chicken to the salad to turn it into a more substantial lunch. Use basil or sundried tomato pesto instead of the chilli jam for a milder flavour.

PENNE PASTA WITH POACHED SALMON, ROASTED FENNEL AND LEMON MAYONNAISE

This is my absolute favourite salad of all time. It's an ideal salad to have ready in advance. While it's a great starter or main course option to have at a summer brunch or lunch it is also a nice option to take to work with you.

Serves 6

4 portions poached salmon (see below)

12oz/350g penne pasta

2 heads fennel, cut into wedges

Approximately 16 cherry tomatoes

2 red onions, cut into wedges

3 cloves garlic, crushed

A little oil

3-4 tablespoons of lemon mayonnaise (see Edward's handy hint)

1oz/25g grated parmesan cheese

2 tablespoons parsley, chopped

Poached Salmon:

4 portions of salmon (approx 7oz/200g each)

$1/_2$ glass of white wine

Lemon wedges

3-4 sprigs fresh parsley

1 onion, sliced

1 bay leaf

Salt & freshly-ground black pepper

Pre-heat the oven to (180C/350F/Gas Mark 4).

Line a baking tray with parchment. Put the salmon on the tray and season with a little salt and cracked black pepper. Pour the wine over the fish, then scatter the bay leaf, sprigs of parsley, onions and lemon wedges around the tray for additional flavour.

Loosely cover the fish with a piece of parchment and tinfoil and put into the pre-heated oven. Bake in the oven for twenty minutes, until cooked through. When cooked sufficiently the salmon will be firm to the touch. Allow to cool completely on the tray and then break the salmon into bite-sized pieces.

Bring a large saucepan of salted water to the boil. Add a little drizzle of olive oil; this will stop the pasta from sticking. Plunge the pasta into the boiling water and cook, then strain into a large colander, blanch and refresh (see p68). Set aside.

Preheat the oven to 180C/350F/Gas Mark 4.

Place the fennel, red onion, garlic and cherry tomatoes onto a flat baking tray. Season with a little salt and pepper, drizzle with a little oil and place in the preheated oven and roast for 20-25 minutes or until all of the vegetables have softened completely. Allow the vegetables to cool.

Mix the roasted vegetables, poached salmon and the chilled pasta together.

Mix in some seasoning and the lemon mayonnaise and stir until it has completely coated all of the pasta and vegetables. Arrange in a large serving bowl and scatter with the grated Parmesan cheese and the chopped parsley.

EDWARD'S HANDY HINT: To make the lemon mayonnaise just mix some mayonnaise with a little chopped parsley and some grated lemon zest

MOROCCAN COUSCOUS

Couscous can be quite a bland ingredient, but if you add the right flavours you can transform it into a really wonderful fresh salad option.

Serves 6

7oz/200g couscous
14floz/400ml boiling water
3oz/75g sultanas/currants
1 small courgette, grated
1 small carrot, grated
16 cherry tomatoes, halved
4 stem spring onions/scallions, chopped
3oz/75g dried apricots, diced
2oz/50g walnuts, chopped
Zest & juice of 1 lemon
$\frac{1}{2}$ teaspoon chilli flakes
$\frac{1}{2}$ teaspoon ground cumin
3 tablespoons oil
2 tablespoons mint, chopped
Salt & freshly-ground black pepper, to season

Place the couscous into a large mixing bowl and cover with boiling water. Leave to stand for ten minutes then gently fluff up with a fork and allow to cool down for about half an hour.

Add in all remaining ingredients and mix well.

Season lightly with salt and black pepper to taste.

Store in the fridge until required.

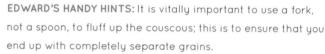

EDWARD'S HANDY HINTS: It is vitally important to use a fork, not a spoon, to fluff up the couscous; this is to ensure that you end up with completely separate grains.

If you wish to add further flavour to the couscous, you could add in some torn lemongrass stalks or thyme sprigs with the boiling water to allow the flavours to infuse into the couscous.

POTATO SALAD WITH PESTO PINE NUTS AND SMOKED BACON

I love potato salad of all varieties and I also love experimenting with potato salads by adding different flavours and combinations. This one is a particular favourite of mine and because it is so quick to make it has appeared at several of my impromptu summer barbecues.

Serves 6

16-20 baby potatoes

A little oil

7 oz/200g smoked bacon lardons

1 red onion, thinly sliced

12-16 cherry tomatoes, halved

3 tablespoons basil pesto

1 tablespoon pine nuts

1oz/25g grated parmesan

Salt & freshly-ground black pepper

Place the baby potatoes into a pan of cold water and bring to the boil. Cook until just tender, strain off the water and allow to steam for a couple of moments. Transfer the potatoes to a large mixing bowl and allow to cool down.

Heat a little oil in a pan and quickly cook the bacon for 3-4 minutes until crispy. Transfer to a small bowl and allow to cool down.

When the potatoes are cold, slice them and add the bacon together with the sliced red onion, cherry tomatoes, pine nuts and seasoning. Drizzle with the basil pesto, mix well and add in a little additional olive oil if required (See Edward's Handy Hints). Sprinkle some grated parmesan over the top and transfer to the fridge until required.

EDWARD'S HANDY HINTS: If you are using shop-bought basil pesto you'll probably need to add the additional oil as they can be quite thick.

If you wish to make your own basil pesto just quickly purée together a large handful of fresh basil with 1 tablespoon pine nuts, 2 tablespoons grated parmesan cheese, juice of $\frac{1}{2}$ lemon, 3 cloves of garlic and 3 $\frac{1}{2}$ floz/100ml olive oil.

SALAD SELECTIONS AND COMBINATIONS

Sometimes when planning a home catering event or a summer barbecue you can be at a loss as to what salads to serve. As well as my favourite salad recipes, which I have included in this chapter, I have also compiled, for your convenience, a series of ingredients that I like to put together to create really tasty salad options. They are not recipes, just suggested combinations that you might like to play around with at home to jazz up your salad repertoire.

Sliced cooked baby potato with crispy smoked bacon and spring onion

Curried rice (rice cooked in curry powder/turmeric with diced raw vegetables and dried fruits)

Traditional coleslaw (shredded white cabbage, grated carrot and mayonnaise)

Sliced baby potato, chorizo, hazelnut and parsley mayonnaise

Diced cucumber, melon, strawberry and mint sprigs

Grated carrot, roasted leek and fennel, olive oil dressing

Quartered tomatoes, rocket and black olive

Couscous with broccoli, mint and lemon zest (don't forget to blanch and refresh the broccoli!)

Grated carrot, apple and sultana with honey and orange juice dressing

New potatoes with mixed herbs, capers and olive oil

Tomato, hard boiled egg, cooked French beans and flat-leaf parsley

Broccoli, hazelnut, cherry tomato and feta cheese (don't forget to blanch and refresh the broccoli!)

Baby spinach, walnuts and feta cheese

Wedges of tomato, roasted peppers, chives and red onion

Cooked noodles, coriander pesto

Poached pear with rocket, blue cheese and walnut

Beetroot wedges, orange segments, spinach leaves & walnut

Apple, celery and walnut with natural yoghurt

Coleslaw with curry powder, apple and pineapple

Grated carrot, peanuts & broccoli (don't forget to blanch and refresh the broccoli!)

Diced cucumber, mint sprigs, yoghurt and dates

DELICIOUS DRESSINGS

Sometimes a dressing can make or break a salad. Here's a series of universal dressings that can be served with large bowls of green salads, vegetable-based salads, crispy bread rolls and barbecued meats.

Chilli Oil:

6 tablespoons olive/rapeseed oil

2 teaspoons crushed chilli flakes

Juice of $\frac{1}{2}$ lime

CHILLI OIL

Whisk all the ingredients together

Mustard Seed:

1 teaspoon wholegrain mustard

1 tablespoon honey

6 floz/175ml olive oil

Juice of $\frac{1}{2}$ lemon

Seasoning

MUSTARD SEED

Put the wholegrain mustard into a large bowl with the honey and lemon juice.
Season lightly with a little salt and pepper.
Whisk the ingredients together until well mixed.
Gradually whisk in the oil until it is well incorporated. The mixture will thicken and emulsify. Store in a screw top jar until required

Tzatziki :

1 cucumber

2 cloves of garlic

2 teaspoons mint, freshly-chopped

2 tablespoons natural yoghurt

Juice of $\frac{1}{2}$ lemon

Cracked black pepper

TZATZIKI

Using a vegetable peeler remove the flesh from the cucumber. It is ok to leave on small pieces of the skin, but do not add any of the seeds to the tzatziki as it will become very soggy.
Add all the other ingredients to the cucumber and mix well until combined.
Store and serve as required.

Summer Herb Dressing:

2 tablespoons mixed herbs, roughly chopped

2 stems spring onions, finely chopped

1 tablespoon capers

Zest and juice of 1 lime

6 tablespoons olive/rapeseed oil

SUMMER HERB DRESSING

Whisk all ingredients together.

Rosemary & Balsamic Infusion:

2 large sprigs of rosemary

1 tablespoon balsamic vinegar

3 cloves garlic, finely chopped

6 tablespoons olive/rapeseed oil

ROSEMARY AND BALSAMIC INFUSION

Whisk all ingredients together.

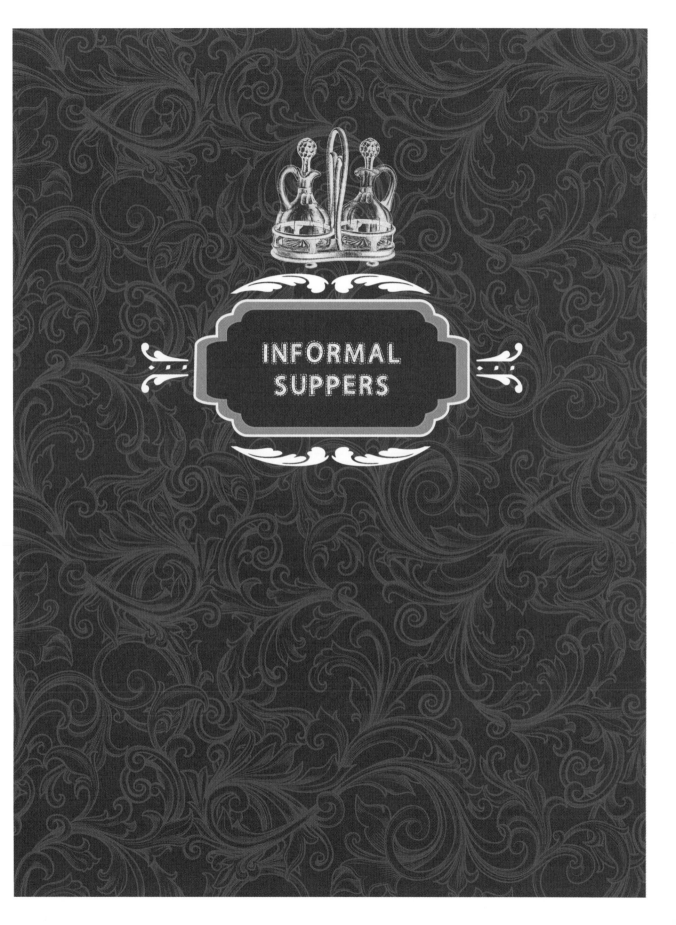

INFORMAL
SUPPERS

CRISPY PORK SALAD WITH CASHEW NUTS AND SWEET POTATO CRISPS

Many Irish people will have pork chops at least once a week. At home one of the biggest weekly problems I have is wondering what treatment to give the humble pork chop. This is a really great salad to have on standby as either a supper option or as a delicious starter at your dinner parties.

Serves 6

Sweet Potato Crisps:
1 large sweet potato
Oil for deep frying

Crispy Pork:
4 pork chops,
$^{1}/_{2}$ teaspoon crushed chilli flakes
2 tablespoons oil

Dressing:
2 tablespoons olive/rapeseed oil
Pinch chilli flakes
Juice of $^{1}/_{2}$ lime
Salt & freshly-ground black pepper

To serve:
Mixed lettuce leaves
16 cherry tomatoes, halved
1 bunch spring onions, chopped roughly
$^{1}/_{2}$ cucumber, thinly sliced
3oz/75g cashew nuts
Chive flowers

SWEET POTATO CRISPS

Peel the sweet potato and using either a sharp knife or a mandolin slice the potato into thin rounds. Heat some oil in a saucepan or alternatively use a deep fat fryer. Check that the oil is hot enough by dropping cubes of white bread into the oil for thirty seconds and allow the bread to become golden brown and crispy. Drop in the slices of sweet potato and cook very quickly for approximately a minute and then carefully drain, with a slotted spoon, onto kitchen paper. Once cool, store in an airtight container until required. They will last for 2-3 days.

CRISPY PORK

Place the pork chops onto your chopping board. Remove all fat from the chops and then using a sharp knife thinly slice/shred the pork into strips.

Mix the shredded pork with the chilli flakes and the oil and leave to marinate for at least a few minutes, preferably a couple of hours, or even overnight.

Heat a large wide-based pan until very hot and then add the pork and marinade and cook quickly, for approximately 4-5 minutes, stirring constantly until the pork is nice and crisp and cooked through.

Drain with a slotted spoon onto some kitchen paper and keep warm until required.

DRESSING

Whisk together all ingredients and store until required.

Mix together the lettuce, tomatoes, spring onion, cucumber and cashew nuts in a large bowl.

Divide between six serving bowls and scatter the crispy pork and the sweet potato crisps on top, drizzle the dressing over the salad, garnish with some edible chive flowers and serve immediately.

SPICED INDIAN PAKORAS

These pakoras make a fantastic vegetarian option for all the family.
A deep-fat fryer is the best option for cooking these pakoras as it's best to have the batter fully immersed in the hot oil. Take care when cooking them though as dropping them into the fryer is quite a precarious task.

Serves 6

Batter:

6oz/175g gram flour (chickpea flour)

1 tablespoon fresh coriander, chopped

Salt & freshly-ground black pepper

1 tablespoon curry powder

$\frac{1}{2}$ red chilli, finely diced

Zest of $\frac{1}{2}$ lime

1 egg

5 floz/150 ml sparkling water

Filling:

$\frac{1}{2}$ courgette, thinly sliced

1$\frac{1}{2}$ peppers, thinly sliced

$\frac{1}{2}$ head cauliflower, broken into small florets

3oz/75g baby spinach

1 onion, thinly sliced

2 carrots, cut into long thin strips

BATTER

Make up the batter by whisking all the ingredients together until a thick yet smooth batter has been achieved. The batter can be left to rest whilst you prepare the vegetables.

FILLING

Mix the sliced vegetables into the batter.

Heat a deep fat fryer. Check that the oil is hot enough by dropping in some cubes of white bread and ensuring that they go golden brown in approximately thirty seconds. Once the oil is hot enough, carefully drop spoonfuls of the mixture into the deep fat fryer and deep fry for 2-3 minutes until the battered vegetables are crispy.

Remove from the hot oil with a slotted spoon and drain on dry kitchen paper. Serve immediately.

EDWARD'S HANDY HINT: When making the batter add the water very sparingly. The mixture, when the vegetables have been added, must be very thick to ensure that the vegetables stick together in the deep fat fryer.

HUNGARIAN BEEF GOULASH

This is a fantastic meal to have simmering on your stove top for entertaining family and friends. The paprika gives a really wonderful flavour to the dish. The beauty of this dish is that, you can make a double batch and freeze some for a later date as it reheats wonderfully.

Serves 6

1lb 8oz/700g stewing beef, cut into chunks

1 large onion, diced

6 cloves garlic, peeled and diced

2 carrots, peeled and cut into chunks

1 red or green pepper, roughly diced

2 teaspoons tomato purée

2 level teaspoons paprika mixed with 1 tablespoon plain flour

1 glass red wine

Dash Worcestershire sauce (optional)

1 can (14floz/400ml) chopped tomatoes

3 tablespoons sour cream

1 pint/600ml beef stock

To serve
Steamed rice & crusty bread

Cut the beef into chunks, ensuring that you trim off any fat.

Heat some of the oil in a large saucepan and add in the diced beef; cook the beef quickly over a high heat until it is browned all over.

Retain the high heat and add in the diced onion, garlic, carrot and red or green pepper and cook these with the beef for a further moment or two.

Next sprinkle in the paprika and flour and coat all of the beef and vegetables in this spice. By frying off the spice in this manner you get a greater intensity of flavour. Add in the tomato puree along with the red wine and Worcestershire sauce, if using.

Next add in the tinned tomatoes, sour cream and the beef stock and stir well. Allow the mixture to come to the boil.

Cover the dish with a tight fitting lid, reduce the heat to a gentle simmer and continue to cook for 1 ½ -1 ¾ hours until the meat is tender.

Serve with some boiled rice and/or some crusty bread rolls.

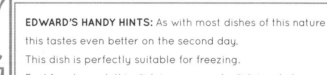

EDWARD'S HANDY HINTS: As with most dishes of this nature this tastes even better on the second day.
This dish is perfectly suitable for freezing.
Feel free to cook this dish in a casserole dish in a hot oven (180C/350F/Gas Mark 4) as another option; it takes the same amount of time.

SPAGHETTI WITH SWEET CHILLI PRAWNS

I spend a lot of my time on the road travelling between work, meetings and cookery demonstrations and its often later in the evening by the time I get home; this is one of my favourite dishes to cook as it is so quick and simple. People often wonder how to cook prawns properly and in this simple recipe I will show you how to serve prawns as either a delicious starter or main course. Feel free to use up leftover cooked chicken in this recipe instead of prawns.

Serves 6

A little oil or butter for cooking

10oz/300g dried/fresh spaghetti

1lb/450g raw prawns (peeled and de-veined)

$^1/_2$ red chilli, diced

$^1/_2$ courgette, diced

1 stick celery, sliced

1 red onion, diced

3oz/75g mixed wild mushrooms, sliced

4 tablespoons sweet chilli jam

2 tablespoon crème fraiche

1 tablespoon flat leaf parsley/coriander, roughly-torn

Juice of $^1/_2$ lemon

Parmesan cheese to serve, optional

Cook the spaghetti according to the instructions in boiling salted water and then strain it through a sieve and leave the cold water running on it so as to refresh it (cool it down).

Meanwhile peel and devein the prawns and retain in the fridge until required.

Heat a wide-based sauté pan with a little oil or butter.

Add in the diced chili, courgette, celery and red onion, together with the sliced mushrooms, and sauté gently until the vegetables are softly cooked.

Increase the heat on the pan and add a little oil as required.

Add in the prawns and cook quickly for about 2-3 minutes until they turn a gentle pink colour.

Pour in the lemon juice, then pour in the crème fraiche and chilli jam and allow these to coat the vegetables and prawns.

Add the cooked spaghetti and mix together to bind all ingredients together.

Tear in the fresh herbs and serve with grated parmesan cheese and cracked black pepper.

EDWARD'S HANDY HINT: Garlic bread is a wonderful accompaniment to this. Why not butter a bread roll with a little garlic butter (p103) and stick it in under the grill.

BEEF AND VEGETABLE NOODLE STIR FRY

This recipe is delicious and is really suitable for family and friends alike.
The stir-fry part of this recipe is also suitable for pork, duck or chicken.

Serves 6

9oz/250g medium egg noodles

1 red chilli, very finely chopped

2 cloves of garlic, chopped

1 $^1/_2$ lb/700g beef sirloin (cut into very thin strips)

1 $^1/_2$ mixed peppers (thinly sliced)

1 medium onion (red or white, thinly sliced)

3oz/75g mange-tout

5-6 mushrooms, sliced

$^1/_2$ teaspoon of ground cumin

4 tablespoons sweet chilli sauce

4 tablespoons soy sauce

Salt & freshly-ground black pepper, to season

Garnish:

2oz/50g cashew nuts

2oz/50g sliced spring onions

Blanch and refresh the noodles by cooking them according to the packet instructions and then straining them into a sieve and leaving them under cold running water until they have completely cooled down. Store in the fridge until required.

Have all of the ingredients prepared in advance because you do need to stand over this dish. Then heat a large saucepan or wok.

Add a little oil to the wok together with the chilli, garlic and sliced beef. Allow the beef to seal off quite quickly. Next add in all of the sliced vegetables (peppers, mushrooms, onions, mange-tout) allow these to cook quickly for approximately 2-3 minutes on a high heat. (See Edward's Handy Hint)

Mix together the sweet chilli sauce and soy sauce.

When the beef and vegetables are almost fully cooked, add in the blanched and refreshed noodles and the sweet chilli sauce and soy mixture and allow to cook for a further 2-3 minutes. Sprinkle in the ground cumin at this stage also.

Correct the seasoning of the dish, garnish with the cashew nuts and spring onions and serve.

EDWARD'S HANDY HINT: Refrain from adding any additional oil to the pan even if your mixture is dry on the pan, it is better instead to use some water or some stock and partially steam everything. This helps to keep your stir-fry from becoming greasy at the end.

PORK AND CIDER STROGANOFF

This dish contains lots of ingredients that are good with pork and will definitely be a favourite with all your family and friends.

Serves 6

A little butter and oil for cooking

2 pork steaks, trimmed
(approximately 2lb/900g)

1 large onion, roughly diced

8 mushrooms, sliced

1oz/25g plain flour

$\frac{1}{2}$ teaspoon of paprika/cayenne
pepper

10 floz/300ml cider

3 $\frac{1}{2}$ floz/100ml pouring cream

14 floz/400ml chicken stock/
water

2 teaspoons wholegrain
mustard

1 large cooking apple, diced

Salt & freshly-ground black
pepper, to season

To serve:
Basmati rice
Fresh parsley, chopped

Melt the butter in a large sauce pan and add a tiny amount of oil to stop the butter from burning. Dice the pork steaks into small pieces, add them to the pot and quickly seal the pork all over. Don't worry about any little pieces of pork that may stick to the base of the saucepan because they will come away later on when you are making your sauce. After the pork is sealed all over season the meat with a little salt and pepper and add the onion and mushrooms and cook gently.

At this stage, sprinkle in the flour and use this to coat the pork and vegetable mixture. If you wish, you can take it off the heat to stir in the flour. Add the paprika or cayenne pepper at this stage.

Return the saucepan to the heat and then pour in the cider, pouring cream and chicken stock. Immediately mix in the wholegrain mustard.

Allow this sauce to come to the boil and then add the chopped cooking apple and reduce the heat to a gentle simmer for a further 30-35 minutes.

Serve the pork and cider stroganoff with some softly-boiled basmati rice. Chopped parsley can be added to the stroganoff just prior to servicing.

EDWARD'S HANDY HINTS: When cooked this dish can be transferred to a casserole dish and topped with shortcrust pastry and baked in the oven for 20 minutes.

Additional stock or even unsweetened apple juice can be used instead of cider.

BRAISED CHICKEN WITH SMOKED BACON CREAM

This is a stewed/casseroled chicken dish that works very well for an informal party. The beauty of this dish is that you can just bring it to the table and let people help themselves.

Serves 6

A little oil for cooking

6 breasts chicken (skin on)

1oz/25g butter

12 small shallots, peeled but left whole

8 mushrooms, sliced

4 rashers of bacon, diced roughly or 4oz/110g smoked bacon lardons

1oz/25g plain flour

$^1/_2$ glass white wine

10 floz/300ml milk/cream (I normally use a combination)

10 floz/300ml good-quality, well-flavoured chicken stock

$^1/_2$ teaspoon wholegrain mustard (optional)

Salt & freshly-ground black pepper, to season

Preheat the oven to 180C/350F/Gas Mark 4.

Heat a little oil in a large pan. Season the chicken breasts with a little salt and pepper and then seal them off on the hot pan until the skin of the chicken is golden brown.

Transfer the chicken from the pan to an ovenproof casserole dish while making the sauce.

Heat the butter in the pan and add the shallots and sliced mushrooms together with the rashers of bacon/bacon lardons. Cook these for 5-6 minutes or until they are just beginning to colour.

Scatter in the flour, making sure to coat everything, then carefully pour in the white wine and stir. Add the chicken stock and the milk or cream. If you are using the wholegrain mustard then add this now too. Allow the sauce to come to a gentle boil and then simmer until it has thickened.

Pour the sauce over the chicken, then cover the dish with a lid/tin foil and transfer to the oven and bake for 40-50 minutes and then remove the lid and bake for an additional 15-20 minutes.

You could serve this with some crisp vegetables and crunchy roast potatoes.

EDWARD'S HANDY HINT: If you wish you can dice this chicken up into small pieces, fry it off with the bacon and mushrooms etc, continue to cook it for a shorter period on the stove top and use it as a chicken casserole to serve with creamy potatoes, rice or pasta.

WHOLE ROASTED CHICKEN LEMON, COURGETTE AND PINE NUT STUFFING

Serves 4-6

1 large free-range chicken
Salt & freshly-ground black pepper
2oz/50g butter

Lemon, Courgette & Pine Nut Stuffing:
3oz/75g butter
1 large courgette, grated
1 medium red onion, roughly diced
Grated zest of 1 lemon
2 tablespoons pine nuts
2 tablespoons parsley, freshly chopped
7oz/200g white breadcrumbs
Salt & freshly-ground black pepper

There is something so special about the smell of a Sunday roast. We often had roast chicken at home and since we were a family with five children we rarely had leftovers!!
Of all of the various methods of roast chicken I've tried over the years this is my favourite. The lemon gives a delicious flavour to the stuffing and of course the grated courgette gives wonderful moisture to the bird. Why not use this stuffing in pork steaks or even chicken breasts wrapped in bacon as a tasty alternative?

First make the stuffing. Melt the butter in a medium saucepan and add the diced red onion and courgette. Cook over a very low heat for 5-6 minutes until all of the ingredients have softened completely. Mix in the lemon zest, pine nuts, freshly-chopped parsley and the soft white breadcrumbs. Season this mixture lightly. Allow to cool down completely.

Preheat the oven to 200C/400F/Gas Mark 6.

Line the cavity of the chicken with some parchment paper and then stuff with the cold stuffing and secure the flap with a cocktail stick. Place the chicken onto a roasting tray, loosen its skin and, taking the butter, gently rub the butter into the breasts of the chicken. Sprinkle a little bit of salt and black pepper over the skin. If you wish, you can cut the lemon you used for the stuffing into large wedges and roast them with the chicken.

Transfer the chicken to the oven and roast for 25-30 minutes. At this stage reduce the temperature of the oven (170C/325F/Gas Mark 3) and cook for a further hour or until the juices run clear out of the chicken. The flesh (particularly on the leg and thigh) should feel tender.

ITALIAN BAKED CHICKEN

This is a great prepare-ahead dish to have for a supper party. Occasionally I have a few friends around for a main course and a glass of wine in the middle of the week; I would serve something like this and rather than concerning myself with elaborate presentation I simply plonk the casserole dish in the middle of the table with a basket of crusty bread and a bowl of green salad and let everyone help themselves.

Serves 6

6 portions of chicken on the bone (legs, thighs, breast can be used)

1 tablespoon oil

2 large onions, roughly sliced

1 courgette, cut into rough chunks

1 1/2 mixed peppers (red, green, yellow)

6 cloves garlic, crushed

3 large plum tomatoes, quartered

1 tablespoon white wine vinegar

3 sprigs thyme

1 teaspoon tomato purée

1 teaspoon caster sugar

10 floz/300ml chicken stock

Salt & freshly-ground black pepper, to season

2oz/50g grated parmesan, to garnish

Herbs like basil or parsley, freshly-chopped, to garnish

Preheat the oven to 170C/325F/Gas Mark 3.

Season the chicken pieces with salt and pepper.

Heat the oil in a large pan, add the chicken and brown on both sides for 2-3 minutes.

Transfer the chicken portions to a casserole dish.

Next add in the sliced onion, mixed peppers, courgette and garlic to the hot pan and continue to cook the mixture for a further 4-5 minutes until the onions and other vegetables are browned.

Next add in the tomato purée, thyme leaves and the tomatoes and allow these to soften a little.

Mix together the vinegar, caster sugar and chicken stock and pour this onto the pan. allow this mixture to come to the boil then transfer to the casserole dish, cover with some tinfoil or a tightly fitting lid and cook for 1 ¼ hours.

Just before serving sprinkle with some grated parmesan and some fresh herbs

Serve with crusty bread and some salad leaves.

EDWARD'S HANDY HINTS: If you like your food spicy, feel free to add in a level teaspoon dried chilli flakes with the vegetables for a spicy taste.

This dish works wonderfully with pork chops also.

SPICED CHICKPEA BROTH

This is a delicious soup as it can be as strongly or as mildly spiced as you wish. It is important to use a good-quality stock in this soup. Made a little thicker this spiced chickpea mixture is nice served with plain boiled basmati rice. Because it is such a filling and chunky option it's perfect for those evenings when you are just looking for something lighter after perhaps having a substantial lunch in the middle of the day.

Serves 6

1 large onion, chopped
1 inch root ginger, chopped
1 red chilli, finely chopped
4 cloves of garlic, crushed
2 sticks of celery, chopped
1 leek, diced
2lb/900g tinned chickpeas
(2 cans)
$^1/_2$ teaspoon of turmeric
1 teaspoon of ground cumin
14floz/400ml/1 tin of chopped
tomatoes
1$^1/_2$ pints/900ml chicken or
vegetable stock/water
2 tablespoons coriander,
chopped
Juice of 1 lime

To Serve
A little natural yoghurt
Flat-leaf parsley

Drain the chickpeas and rinse with cold water.

Chop the leek, onion and celery into small bite-size pieces.

In a large pot heat a little sunflower oil and add the diced leek, celery, onion, ginger, garlic and red chilli. Cook the mixture over a medium heat for 5-6 minutes, or until the vegetables have begun to soften.

Next add in the chickpeas, followed by the turmeric and cumin and allow these spices to infuse with the vegetables for a further 5-6 minutes on a gentle heat.

Pour in the chopped tomatoes and the stock and bring the entire mixture to a boil.

Simmer gently until all of the vegetables are tender.

Season with a little salt and pepper and the juice of the lime and finally add in the freshly-chopped coriander.

Garnish with a little natural yoghurt and flat leaf parsley.

Serve piping hot with very crusty bread.

ROASTED CARROT AND GINGER SOUP

This is a wonderful recipe for soup as it has a nice deep ginger flavour. I like to make it on a cold winter's day and if left to rest for an hour of two or even overnight the flavours of ginger mature.

Serves 6-8

$^1/_2$ medium onion,
roughly chopped
2 inch fresh ginger, roughly
chopped
1oz/25g butter
6 large carrots, peeled and cut
into chunks
1 leek, washed and sliced
2 sticks celery, washed and
sliced
1 large potato, peeled and diced
1 tablespoon honey
2 pints/1200ml vegetable stock/
water
Salt & freshly-ground black
pepper

To Serve:
Natural yoghurt or crème
fraiche
Thyme

In a large saucepan place the chopped onions and ginger, together with the butter, and sauté over a very low heat for 4-5 minutes or until the onions and ginger have softened completely, but are still without colour.

Add in the chopped carrots, leeks, celery and potato, mix well and allow the vegetables to cook in the pan for another 4 or 5 minutes.

At this stage, mix in the honey and allow this to glaze and caramelize the vegetables. Season lightly with a little salt and pepper.

Pour in approximately 1 ½ pints/900ml water or vegetable stock now. (I tend not to add the full water content now just in case. I like to leave some to adjust the consistency of the soup at a later stage. Retain about 10floz/300ml and see if you need to use it.) Bring the mixture to the boil and then to a slow simmer for 20-30 minutes or until the vegetables are fully cooked or softened. With a hand blitzer, puree the soup to a nice smooth consistency. Adjust the consistency with the retained stock to thin the soup if you prefer the soup a little thinner.

Return the soup to the heat. Correct the seasoning as required. Ladle into warmed bowls and serve with a little of natural yoghurt or crème fraiche and a sprig of thyme to garnish

SMOKED HADDOCK CHOWDER

Chowder is such a quick and comforting dish and I just love this smoked haddock option. I always use the undyed smoked haddock for this, but if you can't get it the dyed version works well too.

Serves 6-8

1oz/25g butter

2 sticks celery, diced

1 leek, thinly sliced

1 carrot, diced

1 large potato, cubed

2 cloves garlic, crushed

2 sprigs thyme

1 tablespoon plain flour

$^1/_2$ glass white wine

14floz/400ml fish stock (see below)

9floz/250ml pouring cream

$1^1/_2$/700g lb smoked haddock, diced (preferably undyed)

Salt & freshly-ground black pepper

1 tablespoon basil/tarragon/rosemary, chopped

Simple Fish Stock:

Skin from the fish

1 stick of celery

3 black peppercorns

1 bay leaf

Stalks of fresh parsley

1 wedge of lemon

Water

Heat a large shallow-based sauté pan and sauté the leeks, celery, carrot and potato in the butter with the garlic and thyme until they are glazed, but without colour. Sprinkle in the flour and mix well.

Add in white wine and fish stock together with cream and allow the mixture to come to the boil and then reduce the heat to a gentle simmer and cook, over a medium heat, for approximately ten minutes or until the vegetables have almost fully softened.

When the vegetables have softened add the smoked haddock. At this stage try not to stir the chowder too much as this will cause the fish to break up.

Cook, very gently, for 5-6 minutes until the fish is cooked.

Just after the fish is lightly poached add in some freshly-chopped basil, tarragon or rosemary, together with some salt & freshly-ground black pepper if required. Serve immediately.

SIMPLE FISH STOCK

Bring the entire mixture to the boil for 10 minutes.

EDWARD'S HANDY HINT: If you have no time to make up your own stock use a very mild fish, chicken or vegetable stock cube instead.

GARLIC AND ROSEMARY-SMEARED LAMB CUTLETS WITH GARLIC SAUTÉD POTATOES

Sometimes you are just looking for something a little extra special for a quick midweek meal. Take note if you are planning on getting a little amorous after supper, with six cloves of garlic, this is definitely not the dish for you!

Serves 6

Garlic & Rosemary-Smeared Lamb Cutlets:
12 lamb cutlets
6 cloves garlic
2 large sprigs rosemary, woody stems removed
2 tablespoons oil
Cracked black pepper

Garlic Sautéd Potatoes:
A little oil for cooking
12-16 baby potatoes, thinly sliced
4 cloves garlic, crushed

Garlic & Herb Butter:
2oz/50g butter, softened
2 cloves garlic, chopped
1 tablespoon, parsley, freshly chopped

GARLIC AND ROSEMARY-SMEARED LAMB CUTLETS
Preheat the oven to 200C/400F/Gas Mark 6.
Place the garlic, rosemary, oil and black pepper into a food processor and blend until a coarse consistency has been achieved. Place the lamb cutlets into a large bowl, add the garlic and rosemary puree and mix well.
Heat a large pan with a little oil or butter.
Cook the lamb chops on both sides, on a medium to high heat for approximately 2-3 minutes and then transfer to the oven until required or until they are cooked to your liking. After approximately 5-6 minutes each side in the oven they will be medium. It will take approximately 10-12 minutes for well-done chops.
Serve the lamb chops on top of the garlic sautéed potatoes.

GARLIC SAUTÉD POTATOES
Heat a large wide based pan with a little oil. Add in the thinly-sliced baby potatoes and the crushed garlic and cook over a medium heat, stirring occasionally, until the potatoes are cooked through. Sprinkle with a little chopped parsley before serving.

GARLIC AND HERB BUTTER
Mix the chopped parsley, crushed garlic and softened butter together.
Chill until required and then serve generously on top of the lamb.

EDWARD'S HANDY HINTS: When buying the lamb cutlets ask your butcher to French trim them from the rack for you.
Roll any leftover garlic butter in parchment paper and store in the freezer until required.

FOOD FOR
ROMANCE

GUACAMOLE WITH HOME-BAKED SPICED TORTILLA CRISPS

Avocados have long featured in the top-ten list of aphrodisiacs, so for a romantic night in you can whip up a little avocado dip and serve with some home-made spiced tortilla crisps to give yourself and your special someone something to nibble on!

Serves 6

1 ripe avocado
1 tablespoon coriander or flat-leaf parsley, chopped
Juice of $\frac{1}{2}$ lemon
$\frac{1}{2}$ red chilli, very finely chopped
Salt & freshly-ground black pepper
$\frac{1}{2}$ small red onion, diced
2 plum tomatoes, deseeded and diced
1 tablespoon of mayonnaise, optional

Tortilla crisps:
6 flour tortilla wraps
Approximately 2 tablespoons sunflower oil
Pinch of cayenne pepper or paprika

To make the guacamole add the ingredients (except the tomatoes, red onion and mayonnaise) to a food processor and blitz (or you can blend them in a large bowl using a hand-held blender) until a relatively smooth purée has been achieved. Remove from the blender and mix in the mayonnaise, diced red onion and chopped tomatoes. Make sure it's well chilled before serving.

TORTILLA CRISPS

Preheat the oven to 190C/375F/Gas Mark 5.
Brush each side of the tortilla wraps lightly with oil.
Sprinkle a little paprika or cayenne all over them – not too much as you don't want them to be too hot to eat.
Cut the tortilla wraps into 8-10 wedges and arrange on a baking sheet, making sure not to let them overlap.
Bake for 6-8 minutes in the oven – keep an eye on them as they crisp up quite quickly. Allow to cool. These will keep fresh in an airtight container for up to a week

EDWARD'S HANDY HINT: If you feel very daring use chilli powder instead of the paprika or cayenne for an even hotter taste.

SALAD OF ROASTED FIGS, GORGONZOLA CHEESE AND PARMA HAM

This is a delicious salad, which works wonderfully as part of a light summer dinner party. The advantage, of course, is that you can have these prepared in advance and bake when required.

Serves 2

2 figs

2oz/50g gorgonzola cheese

4 slices Parma ham

Mixed lettuce leaves

Dressing:

2 tablespoons olive oil

1 tablespoon balsamic vinegar

Preheat oven to 190C/375F/Gas Mark 5.

Using a sharp knife, cut each fig in four leaving the base attached so that the fig can be opened out but not separated.

Break the gorgonzola cheese into two evenly-sized pieces, then push a piece into the cavity of each fig and seal back up again.

Meanwhile place the parma ham onto a flat baking tray and place in a preheated oven for 8-10 minutes to allow it to crisp up. When the ham has crisped up, remove from the oven – leave the oven on as you will need it for the figs – allow to cool down and then break into shards.

Place the stuffed figs onto a baking tray and bake for 8-12 minutes until they begin to soften and the cheese starts to melt.

Mix the salad leaves with the dressing and arrange on serving plates.

Garnish with the crisp Parma ham shards.

BEEF STROGANOFF

Fillet of beef is a popular option for romantic nights in and this dish is just the perfect portion and potion for two lovebirds!

Serves 2

1lb /450g fillet of beef

A little oil for cooking

4oz/110g mixed wild mushrooms

2 shallots, sliced

2 cloves garlic, crushed

2 tablespoons brandy

$^{1}/_{2}$ teaspoon paprika

9floz/250ml sour cream

$^{1}/_{2}$ teaspoon wholegrain mustard

3oz/75g gherkins, sliced, to garnish

Flat-leaf parsley, to garnish

Salt & freshly-ground black pepper

Slice the beef into thin strips and place in a large bowl.

Heat the oil in a large heavy-based frying pan until the pan is smoking hot. Add the beef to the hot pan and cook quickly, stirring constantly until it is browned all over.

Add the mushrooms, sliced shallots and crushed garlic and allow them to cook for 3–4 minutes until they, in turn, begin to brown.

Pour in the brandy, bearing in mind that it could ignite, so ensure there is nothing flammable over the pan! Next stir in the paprika, sour cream and wholegrain mustard and allow this entire mixture to come to the boil.

Simmer for 3–4 minutes, or until the sauce has thickened, add salt and pepper to season and serve. Garnish with some chopped flat-leaf parsley and the gherkins if desired.

Serve with garlic sautéed potatoes (p103).

TANDOORI SALMON, SPICY MANGO AND CUCUMBER SALSA

A beautiful, light, tasty option if you're in the mood for a quick romantic supper. The marinade for the salmon is hot and spicy and the mango is said to be a natural aphrodisiac so this dish is perfect for a romantic night in!

Serves 2

1 tablespoons plain yoghurt
2 cloves garlic, crushed
$1/_2$ tablespoon tandoori or other Indian curry paste
Juice of $1/_2$ lemon
$1/_2$ inch ginger, grated
$1/_2$ teaspoon chilli powder
2 fillets of salmon

Salsa:
$1/_2$ mango, peeled and finely chopped
$1/_2$ small cucumber, finely chopped
$1/_2$ red onion, finely chopped
1 medium green chilli, deseeded and finely chopped
1 tablespoon mint, finely chopped
Juice of half a lemon
Pinch chilli powder
Salt & freshly-ground black pepper, to season

To Serve:
Basmati rice
Natural yoghurt
$1/_2$ tablespoon chopped coriander

Preheat the oven to 190C/375F/Gas Mark 5.

Mix the yoghurt, garlic, tandoori curry paste, lemon juice, ginger and chilli powder together in a small bowl and season. Spread over the salmon and chill for at least 20 minutes.

While the salmon is chilling, mix the mango, cucumber, red onion and green chilli together in a small bowl. Add the chopped mint, lemon juice, chilli powder and seasoning and set aside.

Put the chilled salmon on a flat baking tray lined with parchment paper and bake in the preheated oven until blackened at the edges, about 15-20 minutes depending on the thickness of the fish.

Serve with basmati rice, yoghurt, coriander and the mango and cucumber salsa.

CHOCOLATE AND HAZELNUT TERRINE

This gives a real wow factor, so why not give it a try if you really want to impress your date? Take your time making and assembling it – it is well worth the effort.

Makes 8-10 slices

8 digestive biscuits
4oz/110g shelled hazelnuts (or 4 extra digestive biscuits)
1oz/25g melted butter, approx
14oz/400g dark chocolate
5oz/150g milk chocolate
10floz/300ml whipped cream
3 tablespoons liquid glucose

To make this terrine, we will pour a chocolate mousse mixture into a crumb lined terrine mould or loaf tin. In order to get the terrine out in one piece, you need to line it carefully – it does take a little time so don't rush!!

Select a 2lb/900g terrine mould, but you can also use a 2lb/900g loaf tin and brush the mould lightly with melted butter. Neatly line the mould with baking parchment or cling film, making sure that every part of the mould is covered. If using baking parchment you may need to one thick piece going from side to side and a thinner piece going from top to bottom.

In a food processor blitz the digestive biscuits with the hazelnuts until a fine crumb has been achieved. Next prepare the mould for the addition of the crumb coating; brush melted butter all over the lining of the tin / mould, then put in approximately two-thirds of the crumb mixture and shake the mixture all over the inside of the tin trying to ensure that the sides of the tin are lined completely. If needs be you might have to dab a little more melted butter on any patches/uncovered areas and reapply a little crumb. Shake out the excess and put the lined tin in the fridge to set whilst you are making up the chocolate mousse.

Bring a large saucepan of water to the boil. In a large bowl place the dark and milk chocolate and place it over a pot of simmering water. When the chocolate has begun to melt whisk in the liquid glucose and continue to whisk until it is completely melted. Allow the mixture to cool down slightly. Meanwhile carefully fold the whipped cream into the melted (and slightly cooled) chocolate mixture and pour that into the crumb-lined loaf tin until it is almost full to the top. Scatter the remainder of the crushed biscuit & hazelnut mixture on the top. Tap lightly on the work surface to ensure that it is all level and then transfer to the fridge, preferably overnight, but for at least a couple of hours.

TO SERVE

Remove the terrine from the fridge and carefully remove it from the tin by pulling gently on the parchment paper or cling film to ease it from the tin. Warm a large sharp knife and carefully cut into the terrine. It is best to wash and re-warm the knife each time you cut a slice.

EDWARD'S HANDY HINT: If you are having difficulty removing the terrine from the tin then just sit it (very briefly) into a basin of hot water, which will help it to slip out of the tin.

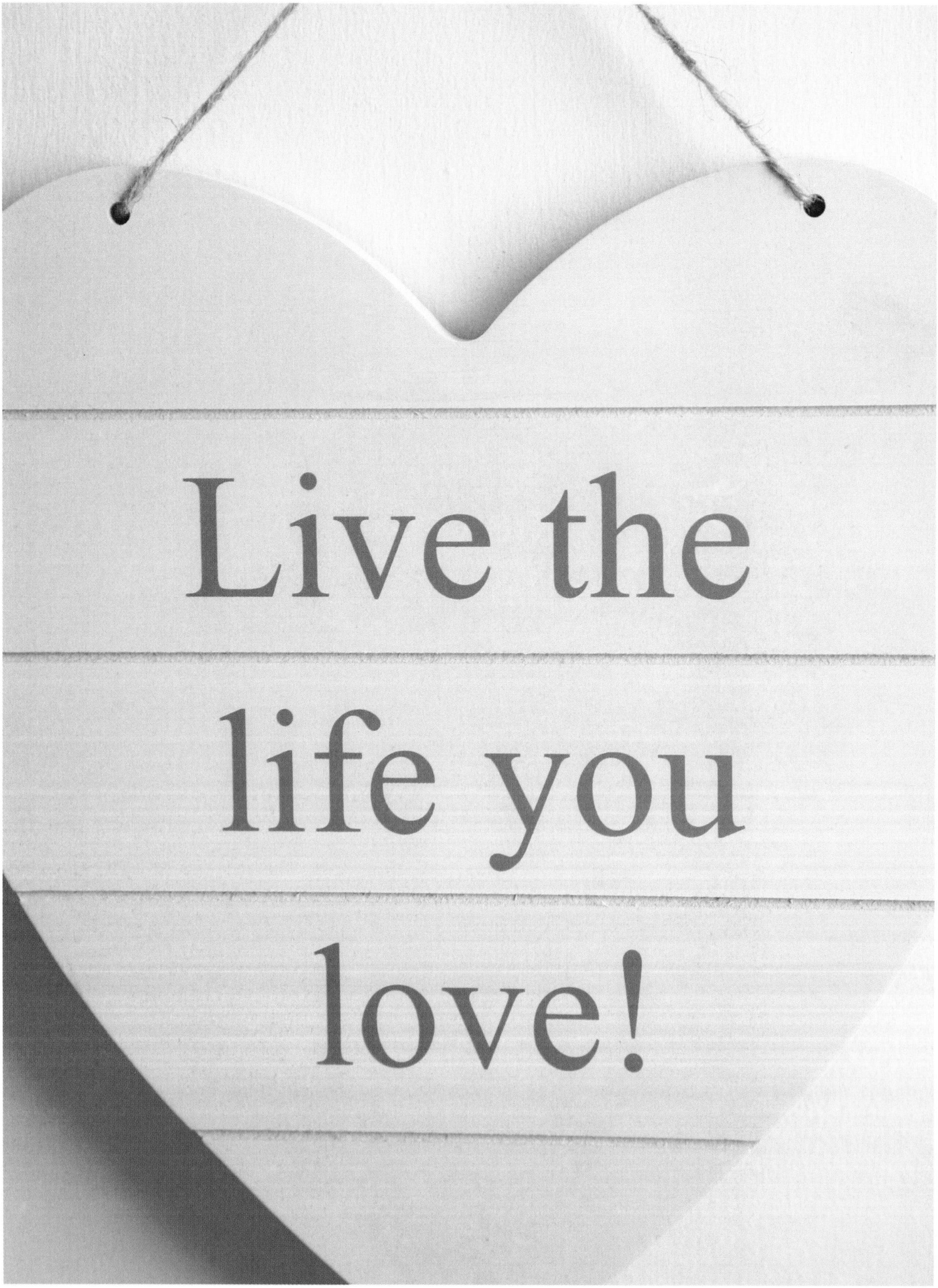
Live the
life you
love!

MOVIE
NIGHT IN

SPICY CHICKEN QUESADILLAS

If you are looking for something quick and tasty to prepare for a girls' or boys' night in, well this is the perfect option. Feel free to vary the fillings!

Serves 6

7oz/200g cheddar or
mozzarella cheese, grated

6oz/175g cooked chicken

1 red onion, very finely diced

4-5 stems spring onions,
chopped roughly

$^1/_2$ red pepper, deseeded &
chopped

2 tablespoons chilli jam/sauce

1 tablespoon chopped parsley

6 medium soft flour tortillas

Salt & freshly-ground black
pepper

In a large mixing bowl mix the cheese, chicken, red onion, spring onion and red pepper together.

Add the chilli sauce and chopped parsley, then season lightly with a little salt and pepper.

Lay the flour tortillas out on the work surface and divide the filling between them. Place another tortilla wrap on top of the mixture and press down firmly to make a sort of sandwich.

Cut the quesadillas in quarters and refrigerate for a couple of minutes to make sure that they remain firm and not liable to lose their cheesy filling.

Gently heat a large pan and brush it with a tiny amount of oil. Fry the quesadilla wedges for two minutes on either side and serve immediately

CRISPY BEEF SPRING ROLLS

Why not take on the takeaway and make your own at home! I love spring rolls so I've got into the habit of having some in my freezer to cook as an impromptu snack. They're perfect to have when friends come round. You can bake these in the oven, but you do get a better finish by deep frying.

Makes 8

7oz/200g fillet beef

$^1/_2$ red chilli, finely diced

2 cloves garlic, chopped

1 carrot, cut into thin strips

$^1/_2$ leek, cut into thin strips

$^1/_2$ red onion, cut into thin strips

$1^1/_2$ mixed peppers, cut into thin strips

2 tablespoons oyster sauce

Additional requirements:

8 sheets spring roll pastry/ wrappers

Egg wash (1 egg mixed with 1 tablespoon milk)

Heat a large wok with a little oil.

Thinly slice the beef and add it to the wok with the chilli and garlic. Stir fry it for 2-3 minutes before adding the vegetables and continue cooking for a further 2-3 minutes or until all are cooked through. Then add the oyster sauce.

Remove from pan and allow to cool down completely.

The mixture must be completely cold before adding it to the spring roll pastry. Place a sheet of spring roll pastry onto a flat surface and brush completely with the egg wash.

Place some of the beef and vegetable mixture towards the bottom of the pastry. Fold in the excess pastry on either side and then roll the spring roll, very tightly, like a Swiss roll, until it is into a tight cylindrical shape.

Heat a deep fat fryer and deep fry the spring rolls for 3-4 minutes until the pastry is completely crisp, they will usually rise to the top of the fryer when they are cooked.

Drain onto some kitchen paper and serve with sweet chilli jam.

EDWARD'S HANDY HINTS: Spring roll pastry is available in any Asian food shop or market.

Alternatively you can use filo pastry. If you are using filo pastry you will need to use two layers together.

Feel free to use leftover cooked chicken or duck instead of the beef or just use a greater selection of vegetables for a vegetarian alternative.

If you do not have a deep fat fryer, you could preheat the oven to 190C/375F/Gas Mark 5, place the spring rolls on a baking tray, brush lightly with a little oil and bake for approximately 18-20 minutes until crisp and golden brown.

CRISPER THAN CRISP POTATO WEDGES

These are such a versatile option to have with any meal. If you are just looking for something savoury and quick on a night in with friends, then these homemade wedges with some chutneys and dips would be the perfect option.

Serves 4

6 large potatoes (I normally use roosters)

1 tablespoon Cajun spice

2 tablespoons oil

Preheat the oven to 190C/375F/Gas Mark 5.

Line a large baking tray with parchment paper.

Wash and dry the potatoes and cut into chunky wedges.

Place the potatoes into a large bowl and drizzle with the oil and Cajun spice, mix everything together then place on the lined baking tray.

Bake for 35-40 minutes until crispy on the outside and well cooked through to the centre. Turn once during the cooking process to ensure even cooking.

Serve immediately with some crème fraiche and chutney.

PITTA PIZZAS

Homemade pizza can be quite demanding on people's time so I've devised this 'cheat's' version which is quick and easy to prepare if time is precious. Sometimes if I were throwing a child's birthday party I would have all the ingredients chopped and prepared separately and allow each child to build their own pizza as a 'party game'. It's just as suitable for adults, and is a fun way to spend an evening in together.

Makes 8

8 mini pitta breads
5oz/150g tomato passata
6-8 mushrooms, sliced
3oz/75g sliced chorizo, sliced
3oz/75g bacon lardons
1 small red onion, sliced
5oz/150g cheddar/mozzarella
cheese, grated

Preheat the oven to 200C/400F/Gas Mark 6.
Line a flat baking tray with baking parchment.
Place the pitta breads onto the baking tray and spread with the tomato passata.
Divide the topping ingredients between the pittas and scatter with the grated cheese on top.
Transfer to the oven and bake for a further 10-15 minutes until the cheese is bubbling and everything is well cooked through.
Serve immediately.

QUICHE IN A TIN

Although I love it, I always think quiche is quite time-consuming to make. The whole blind-baking process adds so much time to the affair that now I always make these mini quiches, which require no blind baking and still give that lovely crisp pastry effect. Again this is one of these recipes that you can vary the flavour as much as you like by substituting ingredients.

Makes 12

Short Crust Pastry:
8oz/225g plain flour
4oz/110g butter
Pinch of salt
A couple of tablespoons of ice cold water

Filling:
A little oil for cooking
$\frac{1}{2}$ courgette, cubed
5oz/150g chorizo, thinly sliced
$\frac{1}{2}$ onion, diced
8 mushrooms, thinly sliced
3 large eggs
10 floz/300ml milk
Salt & ground black pepper
4oz/110g cheese, grated

Preheat the oven to 180C/350F/Gas Mark 4.

Lightly grease a twelve-cup deep muffin tray.

Sieve flour into a large mixing bowl and add a pinch of salt. Rub the butter into the flour and salt mixture until it resembles very fine breadcrumbs, then mix in enough ice-cold water to bring the mixture together.

Knead the pastry gently, then cover with cling film and rest in the fridge until required. Roll out the pastry, cut into discs and use it to line the twelve cups of the muffin tray. Heat a little oil in a large, wide-based sauté pan and add the courgette, chorizo, onion and mushrooms and cook over a medium heat until they have softened. Allow these to cool and then divide between the pastry lined cups of the muffin tray.

In a large jug whisk together the eggs with the milk and seasoning. Carefully pour this mixture into the pastry-lined cups, sprinkle with a little cheese and bake in the preheated oven for approximately twenty minutes or until the pastry is crisp, the egg custard has fully set and the cheese is bubbling.

Allow to cool in the tin for five minutes and then, using a palette knife, carefully remove them from the tin and serve, either hot or cold.

EDWARD'S HANDY HINT: Sometimes I replace a little of the milk with some cream for added richness.

PLOTTING AND PLANNING A DINNER PARTY

WHITE SODA SCONES WITH CHEESE AND THYME

I adore these scones as a bread option for a dinner party, but also as a lunchbox filler. You can have as much fun and variation as you like by playing around with the ingredients to change the flavours.

Makes 10-12

Savoury Scone Mixture:
A little butter for greasing
1lb/450g plain flour
1 rounded teaspoon baking powder
$\frac{1}{2}$ teaspoon cayenne pepper or paprika
Pinch salt
3oz/75g butter, diced
3oz/75g cheddar cheese, grated
2 teaspoons of thyme, freshly chopped
1 large egg
Approximately 7floz/200ml buttermilk

Glaze:
1 egg & 3 tablespoons milk, beaten together
Thyme sprigs
A little extra cheddar cheese, grated (optional)

Preheat the oven to 180C/350F/Gas Mark 4.

Lightly grease a flat baking tray.

Sieve the flour, baking powder and cayenne pepper or paprika into a large bowl.

Add the salt and diced butter. Gently rub the butter into the flour.

Add the grated cheese and chopped thyme.

In a separate bowl lightly whisk the egg together and add to the dry ingredients. Mix in the buttermilk to achieve a soft sticky dough.

Roll out on a floured work surface and cut into 10-12 equal-sized shapes using either a sharp knife or a scone cutter.

Brush lightly with the beaten egg and milk and sprinkle with the thyme sprigs, or a little extra cheese if you wish.

Bake in the oven for 20-25 minutes until well-risen and golden.

Serve warm with butter.

EDWARD'S HANDY HINT: You may need to use extra buttermilk to achieve the right consistency.

You could also add other ingredients to the savoury scones such as cooked bacon lardons, chorizo, roasted vegetables or sundried tomatoes.

CREAMY POTATO, LEEK AND THYME SOUP

This soup is a delicious and warming option to begin a winter dinner party. I love to serve my soup in little tea/coffee cups as a quirky serving option, and I always find that it is the right amount of soup, leaving adequate room for main course and dessert.

Makes 6-8

1oz/25g butter
5-6 large potatoes, peeled and chopped
1 celery stick, chopped
2 small leeks, trimmed and sliced
$1/_2$ medium onion, peeled and chopped
2 garlic cloves, peeled and finely chopped
3 large sprigs of thyme
2 pints/1200ml chicken or vegetable stock
5 fl oz/150ml pouring cream
Salt & freshly ground black pepper

Garnish:
Whipped cream
Thyme sprigs

Heat the butter in a large saucepan and toss the chopped potato, celery, leeks, onion and garlic together with the three thyme sprigs. Allow them to cook very gently (and without browning) for 8-10 minutes or until the smaller of the vegetables are glazed. Add about two-thirds of the chicken or vegetable stock to the pan and bring the mixture to a slow boil, then reduce the heat and simmer for 15-20 minutes or until all of the vegetables, including the potatoes, have completely softened.

Remove the pan from the heat and use a hand-held blender to blitz the soup until it is nice and smooth. Stir in the cream, then return to the heat and bring back to a very gentle boil. If you prefer a thinner soup, now is the time to add some of the leftover stock or some cream to thin the consistency.

Season with salt and pepper to taste, then transfer the soup into bowls or cups and garnish with some whipped cream and sprigs of thyme.

Alternatively, if you want to freeze the soup, allow to cool down completely, then transfer into containers and put in the freezer until required.

CROCK OF MUSSELS IN A WHITE WINE AND CREAM BROTH

There is nothing better or nicer than heading off to pick your own mussels, then returning home to cook them up in the simplest way and serve them to your guests as a delicious starter at a dinner party. Alternatively your local fishmonger should have a good selection.

Serves 6

A little oil for frying

1 medium onion, roughly chopped

6 cloves of garlic, crushed

2 lbs 4oz/1.5kg mussels, scrubbed clean & shells closed

¹/₂ glass of dry white wine

10 floz/300ml cream

Juice of half a lemon

Chopped herbs (parsley is ideal)

Cracked black pepper, to season

Some crusty bread or soda bread, to serve

Heat a large wide-based sauté pan or a pot with a little oil and then add in the onion and garlic until nicely browned.

Add in the well-scrubbed mussels ensuring that all shells are closed going in. Toss gently in the onion and garlic mixture.

Now to the indulgence – add the white wine and cream and allow this mixture to come to the boil. Part of the liquid will reduce and part will continue to cook the mussels. Increase the heat to the highest setting and put on a tight-fitting lid. When the majority of the mussels have opened add the lemon juice and chopped herbs. Lightly season the broth with black pepper. Discard any unopened mussels at this stage.

Immediately place the pan in the centre of the table and allow everyone to dig in! Serve with bread.

EDWARD'S HANDY HINTS: The mussels need to be scrubbed well to remove any dirt or grit and also to pull off the beards – the string-like things hanging from the end of mussels. When cleaned, cover with a damp cloth until ready to use and store in the fridge.

Ensure that all mussels are closed going into the pot and open coming out. A sharp tap should close any mussels that have opened whilst washing, if it does not you need to discard the mussel immediately.

SPAGHETTI WITH CRAB MEAT AND CHILLI

Dinner parties give us the added luxury of being indulgent so don't worry about the calorie content of this dish! If you don't particularly like crab why not consider adding some lefto-ver cooked chicken instead?

Serves 6

10oz/300g spaghetti

1 large red onion, finely diced

1 red chilli, deseeded and finely diced

3 cloves garlic, finely diced

7floz/200ml pouring cream

Juice of ½ lemon

8oz/225g freshly-cooked crab meat

Salt & freshly-ground black pepper

2 tablespoons coriander, torn

Parmesan cheese, grated

Bring a large saucepan of water to the boil. Cook the spaghetti according to the packet instructions. Once the spaghetti is cooked, strain it into a colander and leave it under cold running water until completely cool, this will halt the cooking process and stop the spaghetti from sticking together.

Meanwhile, heat a large shallow-based sauté pan with a little oil and add in the diced onion, garlic and chilli and sauté gently for 3-4 minutes, stirring constantly. Next add in the cream and lemon juice and allow the mixture to come to the boil. Season a little with some salt and pepper.

Once the cream has come to the boil mix in the crab meat and stir thoroughly. Add in the cooled spaghetti at this stage and mix well, ensuring the spaghetti is completely coated with the creamy sauce. Continue to cook over a medium heat until the spaghetti piping hot.

Garnish with the torn coriander and serve immediately with some grated par-mesan cheese.

EDWARD'S HANDY HINT: Make sure to pick through the crab meat to ensure there are no traces of shell in the meat.

CRUSTED HAKE WITH CRUNCHY PINE NUT TOPPING

This dish makes a very colourful option for a dinner party and yet it is relatively quick and easy to prepare. The almonds give a lovely crunch to the soft flaky fish. You can substitute cod or salmon for the hake if you prefer.

Serves 6

6 portions of hake (6oz/150g each)
1 lemon, cut into wedges
12-18 cherry tomatoes
6 sprigs fresh thyme
Salt & freshly-ground black pepper

Topping:
2oz/50g butter
4oz/110g breadcrumbs
2oz/50g pine nuts
1 tablespoon parmesan cheese, grated
2 tablespoons fresh herbs, parsley & thyme, chopped
Grated zest of one lemon

Preheat the oven to 180C/350F/Gas Mark 4.

Begin by making the topping: melt the butter and add in the breadcrumbs, grated lemon zest, parmesan cheese, chopped herbs and pine nuts. Allow to cool for a couple of minutes.

Line a roasting tray with baking parchment and place the portions of fish on it. Season the fish with a little salt and freshly-ground black pepper. Press some of the breadcrumb topping onto the top of each piece of fish. Scatter the lemon wedges and cherry tomatoes on the tray and place a sprig of thyme on top of each portion of hake.

Bake for approximately twenty minutes depending on the thickness of the fish; when cooked the fish should be firm to the touch with a crunchy crumble-style topping.

FILLET OF BEEF WITH SAUTÉD SPINACH AND MUSHROOM WITH BLACK PEPPER CREAM SAUCE

Beef is always a crowd-pleaser and this very simple but tasty recipe will be a big hit at any soirée. The sauce can be made up in advance, which is a good time saver on the evening of your dinner party.

Serves 6

Black Pepper Cream Sauce:
2 shallots, finely diced
1 tablespoon flour
10 floz/300 ml beef stock
3 ½ floz/100 ml cream
Whole black peppercorns
(approx 12)
A little oil for cooking

Fillet of Beef:
3 tablespoons oil
3 sprigs thyme
3 cloves garlic, crushed
6 black peppercorns, roughly crushed
6 fillet steaks (approx 7oz/200 g per person)

Mushroom & Spinach with Shallots
5oz/150 g mushrooms
1oz/25 g butter
7oz/200 g baby spinach leaves

BLACK PEPPER CREAM SAUCE

Add the diced shallots to the pot with a tiny amount of oil. Add the peppercorns now also. Sprinkle in the flour.

Pour in the cream and the stock and bring to the boil for approximately 7-10 minutes. Allow this to boil and reduce a little allowing this to reduce to a syrup-style sauce. If you are making the sauce in advance bring it back to the boil before serving.

FILLET OF BEEF

Arrange the steaks in a non-metallic shallow dish.

In a separate bowl, mix together the oil with the thyme sprigs, crushed peppercorns and chopped garlic. Pour this over the steaks, cover the dish with cling film and allow to marinate, in the fridge for at least two hours, but longer if time allows (overnight is fine).

To cook the steaks, heat a large pan or griddle pan.

Add the steaks to the hot pan and – providing they are not too thick – cook them in the following pattern:

Rare: 2 minutes on either side.

Medium: 4 minutes on either side.

Well done: 5 minutes on either side.

SAUTÉD SPINACH AND MUSHROOM

Meanwhile as your steak is cooking, heat another large frying pan with the butter.

Add in the mushrooms and cook on a medium heat for 3-4 minutes and then at the last minute add in the spinach for the final minute or two of cooking time. Season accordingly.

PORK STEAK STUFFED WITH CURRIED RICE

This is a delicious way of cooking and serving the pork steak and will make for a very impressive display at your dinner party. As with lots of the recipes in this section the pork steak can be prepared and stuffed in advance to allow for a stress free evening. It's most unusual, but works very well. Pork by its nature can be a little bland so the curried flavour adds the perfect element of spice.

Serves 4

1 large pork steak
4oz/110g basmati rice
1 tablespoon medium-hot curry powder
3oz/75g chorizo, finely diced
1 red pepper, diced
1 bunch scallions, finely chopped
1oz/25g sultanas
1 tablespoon herbs, finely chopped
Salt & freshly-ground black pepper
1 egg yolk
4 rashers of bacon

Begin by making the curried-rice stuffing. Place the basmati rice into a medium saucepan and cook according to the packet instructions. Once the water has begun to come to the boil add the curry powder and stir thoroughly, ensuring that it is fully combined. When the rice is cooked, strain it into a large sieve and leave under cold running water until it has completely cooled down. Transfer to a medium-sized mixing bowl. Meanwhile, in a shallow frying pan sauté the chorizo and red pepper for 3-4 minutes until the pepper has softened. Allow this mixture to cool down and then add it to the cooked rice. Add in the scallions, sultanas, chopped herbs, salt and freshly-ground black pepper along with the egg yolk. Mix well, ensuring the mixture is fully combined.

Preheat the oven to 180C/350F/Gas Mark 4. Remove the fat and sinew from the pork steak, or alternatively ask your friendly butcher to do this for you. Butterfly the pork steak by splitting it from the side using a very sharp knife. Do not cut through the pork steak fully, but rather leave it open like a book. Place it onto a large chopping board, cover with a double layer of cling film and, using a rolling pin, flatten it well.

Remove the cling film and transfer the pork steak to a single layer of parchment paper. Spread the stuffing along the middle of the pork steak and then neatly roll up. Tightly wrap the rashers around the pork steak to keep the stuffing in place. Using the parchment paper to assist you, wrap the pork roulade – still encased in parchment paper – in tinfoil and twist tightly at each end. Place onto a flat baking tray and bake for half an hour. Then carefully remove the parchment paper and tinfoil and return the pork to the oven for an additional twenty minutes to brown. Once the pork comes out of the oven, cover it tightly with a fresh piece of tinfoil and allow it to rest for at least ten minutes before carving.

This would be tasty served with roasted sweet potatoes and some wilted spinach.

BAKED LEMON SOLE WITH SALSA VERDE

I simply adore the flavour of lemon sole and I think this dish, although it may appear challenging, will definitely be a big hit at your dinner party. If lemon sole is not your fancy it can be replaced with fillets of salmon, cod, haddock or even monkfish for a similar effect.

Serves 6

6 lemon sole on the bone (skin removed)
2oz/50g butter
Parsley, freshly chopped
Juice of 1 lemon
Salt & freshly-ground black pepper

Salsa Verde:
2 tablespoons fresh parsley, roughly chopped
1 tablespoon basil leaves, roughly chopped
1 tablespoon mint leaves, roughly chopped
4 tinned anchovy fillets, diced
1 tablespoon capers, rinsed
2 cloves of garlic, roughly chopped
2 tablespoons white wine vinegar
Pinch sugar
6floz/175ml extra virgin olive oil
Salt & freshly-ground black pepper

Preheat the oven to 190C/375F/Gas Mark 5.

Begin by making the salsa verde; in a medium bowl mix together the parsley, basil & mint with the capers, garlic and anchovies.

In a separate bowl, mix together the olive oil, white wine vinegar, sugar, salt and freshly-ground black pepper. Pour this over the chopped herb mixture and allow to rest for at least half an hour.

Meanwhile line a large baking tray with parchment paper, place the fish on the baking tray, season them lightly with salt and pepper and divide the butter between the six fish, putting a little cube on top of each fish. Squeeze the juice of the lemon over the fish, then bake in the preheated oven for 15-20 minutes until the fish is firm to the touch. When it is cooked sprinkle with the chopped parsley and serve immediately with the salsa verde.

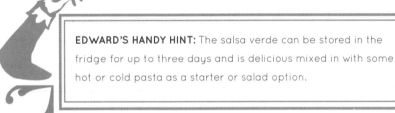

EDWARD'S HANDY HINT: The salsa verde can be stored in the fridge for up to three days and is delicious mixed in with some hot or cold pasta as a starter or salad option.

BAKED GINGER PUDDING, CINNAMON-ROASTED PEARS WITH BUTTERSCOTCH SAUCE

The combination of the rich sauce with the moist, spiced ginger pudding is delicious and is a very indulgent dessert to complete an elaborate dinner party. The roasted pears just add a sense of extravagance. Despite the impressive visual element of this dish it is surprisingly simple to make, which just adds to the appeal!

Serves 6

Pudding:
8oz/225g plain flour
4oz/110g brown sugar
1 rounded teaspoon baking powder
1 teaspoon ground cinnamon
2 teaspoon ground ginger
4oz/110g butter, melted
2 large eggs
1 tablespoon black treacle
3floz/75ml milk

Cinnamon-Roasted Pears:
6 baby pears
2oz/50g caster sugar
1oz/25g butter
1oz/25g brown sugar
Pinch cinnamon

Butterscotch Sauce
2oz/50g butter
2oz/50g brown sugar
7floz/200ml pouring cream

PUDDING

Preheat the oven to 180C/350F/Gas Mark 4.

Grease six individual metal pudding basins or ramekins.

Sieve the flour, baking powder and spices together into a large bowl, then add the brown sugar. Make a well in the dry ingredients and pour in the eggs, melted butter, milk and treacle and whisk until a smooth batter has been achieved.

Divide the mixture between the well-greased pudding basins or ramekins.

Bake for 20-25 minutes at until a skewer inserted in the centre comes out clean. Allow to cool slightly and then invert onto the serving platter.

CINNAMON-ROASTED PEARS

Peel the pears carefully leaving the stalk intact. Place them in a medium saucepan with the caster sugar. Cover with cold water and bring to the boil. Simmer for approximately 5-10 minutes until just tender. Allow to cool.

When you are ready to serve the dessert, heat the butter on a medium-sized ovenproof frying pan, add the brown sugar and a pinch of cinnamon. Melt carefully, then toss in the pears and cook gently, stirring constantly, until they are golden brown. Transfer the pan of pears to the preheated oven for a further 5-10 minutes stirring occasionally until the pears are completely softened. Baste with the liquid caramel in the pan, pour over the butterscotch sauce and serve.

BUTTERSCOTCH SAUCE

Melt the butter and brown sugar until bubbling gently, then whisk in the cream and simmer gently for 5 minutes.

EDWARD'S HANDY HINT: This pudding can be successfully reheated in the microwave. The butterscotch sauce can be kept in the fridge for up to three weeks.

CHOCOLATE TRUFFLE CAKE

This is a lovely rich dessert to conclude your dinner party. Just sit back and watch your guests drool as you bring this sinful delight to the table. For ease of preparation you should have the sponge made the day before you require the chocolate truffle cake so that all you have left to do on the day is to assemble and decorate the cake.

Serves 8-10

Sponge:
8oz/225g butter, softened
8oz/225g caster sugar
8oz/225g self-raising flour
5 medium eggs
1oz/25g good-quality cocoa

Chocolate Truffle Mixture:
1lb/450g chocolate ($^1/_2$ dark and $^1/_2$ milk mixed), chopped into small pieces
5floz/150ml cream
4oz/110g butter, cut into cubes
1 egg yolk
Zest of 1 orange
7oz/200g nibbed almonds

SPONGE

Preheat oven to 180C/350F/Gas Mark 4.

Grease and line an 8 inch/20 cm deep cake tin.

In a large mixing bowl cream the butter with the sugar until very light and fluffy. Gradually add the eggs, then sift the flour and the cocoa powder together and add to the bowl. Mix thoroughly until the mixture is really light and creamy

Pour the mixture into the prepared cake tin and bake for 45-50 minutes or until the cake is well set (a skewer inserted into the centre of the cake should come away spotlessly clean and dry).

When the cake is cooked take it out of the oven and allow it to cool in the tin for at least half an hour as it will still be quite soft.

Invert onto a cooling rack and allow to cool completely.

CHOCOLATE TRUFFLE MIXTURE

Preheat the oven to 190C/375F/Gas Mark 5.

Place the chocolate in a large bowl. Add the butter and cream to a saucepan and allow to come to a rapid boil, then pour the boiling liquid onto the chocolate and whisk rapidly. Add the egg yolk, together with the orange zest and whisk thoroughly. Allow the truffle mixture to cool slightly until it has a spreadable consistency. Meanwhile place the almonds on a flat baking tray and toast them in the preheated oven until golden brown. Allow to cool down.

ASSEMBLY

Split the chocolate sponge in three equal pieces. Spread a layer of chocolate truffle mixture over the first disc of sponge, top it with another disc of sponge and repeat the process. Spread the top and sides of the cake with some of the chocolate truffle mixture. You will need to use about two-thirds of the truffle mixture filling and icing the cake. Pour the remaining mixture onto a flat baking tray lined with cling film and refrigerate for a couple of hours until it is set. When the remaining truffle mixture has set break the chocolate slab into small pieces. Using your hands (I normally use disposable gloves as it can be a messy procedure) manipulate the truffles into round balls and roll in the toasted almonds. Generously decorate the top of the cake with the chocolate truffles.

EDWARD'S APPLE AND RHUBARB CRUMBLE CAKE

This is a most unusual recipe, is it a cake, is it a crumble? Who knows?
What it will be, though, is a wonderful end to your dinner party and because of its unusual
consistency will be a talking point at the table.

Serves 8-10

Cake Mixture:

8oz/225g butter, softened

8oz/225g demerara sugar

4 eggs

1 tablespoon milk (approx)

8oz/225g plain flour

2oz/50g ground almonds

1 rounded teaspoon baking
powder

¹/₂ teaspoon cinnamon

Fruit Filling:

1oz/25g butter

1oz/25g caster sugar

3 eating apples, peeled and cut
into wedges

3 sticks rhubarb, chopped

Crumble Topping:

3oz/75g hard butter

3oz/75g demerara sugar

4oz/110g plain flour

2oz/50g flaked almonds

Pinch cinnamon

1 tablespoon honey

Preheat the oven to 170C/325F/Gas Mark 3.

Grease an 8 inch/20cm deep round cake tin.

Line the base and the sides of the tin with some baking parchment.

FILLING

Heat a little butter in a large frying pan, add in the chunks of apple and rhubarb and cook gently for a couple of minutes.

Add the caster sugar and continue to cook until the sugar has dissolved. You just need to soften (not cook) the apples. Turn off the heat and allow the apple and rhubarb mixture to cool down.

CRUMBLE TOPPING

Sieve the plain flour into a large mixing bowl. Add the sugar and the cinnamon and mix well. Cut the butter into cubes and, using the tips of your fingers, rub this into the flour and sugar mixture. Add in the flaked almonds now and cover until needed.

CAKE MIXTURE

Meanwhile in a large mixing bowl cream the butter and the sugar together until light and fluffy. Add in the eggs and milk. Sieve together the flour, baking powder, ground almonds and cinnamon and add these to the mixture also. Mix well until a creamy consistency has been achieved.

ASSEMBLY

Place approximately half of the cake mixture into the prepared tin. Carefully arrange half of the fruit filling on top of the cake and then sprinkle approximately half of the crumble topping on top of this.

Carefully spread the remaining cake mixture on top of this.

Neatly arrange the rest of the apple and rhubarb on top of the cake and then cover with the remaining crumble.

Bake in the preheated oven for an hour and a half. After the first 45 minutes reduce the oven temperature to 150C/300F/Gas Mark 2, check on the cake and, if the cake is browning excessively, you can cover it with some tin foil or baking parchment.

You'll know the cake is cooked if you insert a skewer into the middle of the cake and it comes out clean.

Allow the cake to cool slightly in the tin and then carefully remove the cake from the tin and place it on a large serving platter.

Drizzle the cake with the honey and serve with some freshly-whipped cream or crème fraiche.

ALL THE
BIG OCCASIONS

PESTO AND SUNDRIED TOMATO BREAD

Bread is such an important part of a meal and with this bread option you can have interesting, flavoured fillings within the bread itself. This is a great tasty bread option and a great way of jazzing up a white soda bread recipe. Feel free to experiment with different flavours.

Makes 1 loaf

A little oil or butter for greasing

1lb/450g plain flour

1 level teaspoon bread soda

$^1/_2$ teaspoon salt

4oz/110g sundried tomatoes, chopped

Approximately 12floz/350ml buttermilk

2 tablespoons basil pesto (see page 75) salad combinations

2oz/50g parmesan cheese, grated

Preheat oven to 170C/325F/Gas Mark 3.

Lightly grease a flat baking tray with a little oil or butter and dust lightly with some plain flour.

Sieve together the flour, bread soda and salt into a large mixing bowl.

Mix in the chopped sundried tomatoes. Make a well in the centre, pour in most of the buttermilk and, using a spoon mix to a soft dough. Sometimes, depending on the moisture content of the sundried tomatoes, you may need to add a little extra milk to bring the mixture together.

Transfer the mixture onto a lightly-floured work surface and flatten gently with a rolling pin into a rough square shape (approximately 9inch/23cm in diameter). Spread the pesto over the dough, sprinkle with the cheese and roll the dough up like a swiss roll.

Carefully transfer the bread onto the previously-lined baking tray and sprinkle the top of the bread with a little plain flour.

Bake for 35-45 minutes approximately until the bread sounds hollow when tapped underneath.

EDWARD'S HANDY HINT: Try using some chopped, roasted vegetables or cheese instead of the sundried tomatoes.

SPICED WINTER VEGETABLE SOUP

This is a very warming, nourishing soup with the ginger giving a nice lightly-spiced flavour to the soup. I always think soup is a great option to have when entertaining at home as you can have it prepared in advance and it is a great 'filler' to serve to guests after an occasion whilst you are getting all the other dishes ready.

Serves 6-8

1oz/25g butter

$^1/_2$ medium onion, chopped

2 sticks of celery, chopped

1 medium leek, washed and sliced

1 sweet potato, peeled and diced

1 medium butternut squash, peeled and cut into chunks

2 medium carrots, peeled and chopped

1 inch fresh root ginger, peeled

3 cloves of garlic, crushed

2 large sprigs of thyme

Salt & freshly-ground black pepper

2 pints/1200ml water

3floz/75ml cream

Pinch ground cinnamon (optional)

Heat the butter in a large saucepan and toss in all the vegetables, together with the ginger, crushed garlic and thyme sprigs. Allow them to cook very gently (and without colour) for 8-10 minutes or until the smaller vegetables are beginning to soften. Next add in approximately two-thirds of the water and bring the mixture to a slow boil and then reduce the heat and simmer for an additional 15-20 minutes or until all of the vegetables have softened completely.

Using a hand blender, blitz the soup until it is nice and smooth. Mix in the cream and ground cinnamon (if using) at this stage and return to the heat and bring back to a very gentle boil. If you would like a thinner soup, now would be the best time to add some additional water to thin it down. Correct the seasoning at this stage also.

Transfer it to your serving bowls or cups and garnish the soup with a little crème fraiche or pouring cream infused with some additional ground cinnamon.

EDWARD'S HANDY HINT: You can allow the soup to cool down and then transfer it into suitable containers and freeze until required.

MEDITERRANEAN VEGETABLE STACK

Vegetarians so often lose out just by getting a plate of vegetables so to make their menu more appealing and inviting I have devised this fantastic recipe.
It is perfect for all your dining requirements.

Serves 6-8

4-5 tortilla wraps
8oz/225g grated mozzarella
cheese

Filling:
A little oil for frying
1 courgette, cut into chunks
1 red onion, cut into chunks
1 red pepper, deseeded and cut
into chunks
1 green pepper, deseeded and
cut into chunks
1 yellow pepper, deseeded and
cut into chunks
6-8 mushrooms, sliced
4 cloves garlic, crushed
$\frac{1}{2}$ teaspoon dried
mixed herbs
2x 14oz/400g tin of
tomatoes (fresh plum
tomatoes could also be used)
Pinch sugar
Salt & freshly-ground black
pepper

Gently heat a little oil in a large pot and fry off the vegetables and crushed garlic until they are all glazed and beginning to soften.

Pour in the chopped tomatoes, sugar and mixed herbs at this stage and allow the mixture to cook very gently on a nice low heat for about 25 minutes.

Season according to taste and allow to cool down.

ASSEMBLY

Lay a tortilla wrap on the base of a flat baking tray lined with baking parchment Cover with some of the vegetable mixture (and some of the grated mozzarella) and repeat this process.

Repeat until approx 4–5 layers have been achieved.

Finish with a tortilla wrap on the top, sprinkled with some of the grated cheese. Heat the oven to 190C/375F/Gas Mark 5 and bake the stack for 15–20 minutes until bubbling hot. Serve with a large green salad.

EDWARD'S HANDY HINTS: The cooked vegetable mixture makes a great vegetable accompaniment for a meal.
The stack can be made up in advance and left in the fridge until ready to bake.

PORK AND CHICKEN TERRINE

This is a delicious option to serve cold as part of a special buffet. It's a fantastic dish to serve if you're planning a party as it actually works and tastes better if you prepare it a couple of days in advance.

Serves 12

Approximately 10-14 rashers of streaky bacon.

2oz/50g ready to eat prunes, finely chopped

1 ¹/₂ lb/700g minced pork

¹/₂ medium onion, finely diced

2 cloves of garlic, chopped

2oz/50g fresh white breadcrumbs

1 egg

Salt & freshly-ground black pepper

1 tablespoon fresh mixed herbs, chopped

1 teaspoon wholegrain mustard

Dash Worcestershire sauce

2 chicken breasts (skinless & boneless)

2oz/50g ready to eat apricots

Mixed salad leaves, to serve

Preheat the oven to 170C/325f/Gas Mark 3.

Line a 2lb/900g loaf tin or terrine mould with bacon, leaving a little overlapping; you'll use this overlap to enclose the terrine.

Mix the prunes, pork mince, onions, garlic and breadcrumbs together with the egg and season lightly. Add in chopped mixed herbs, mustard and Worcestershire sauce. Half fill the terrine mould with the meat mixture.

Slice the chicken into thin strips. Put in a layer of chicken into the terrine mould, then arrange a layer of apricots down the centre.

Put in the remaining meat mixture and close over the smoked bacon overhang. Cover the mould with tinfoil.

Sit the terrine mould into a roasting dish half filled with water and cover the entire tin with tinfoil.

Bake for an hour, remove the tin foil and reduce the heat to 150C/300F/Gas Mark 2 and bake for a further 45 minutes.

Allow to cool in the tin and then invert onto a serving platter and decorate with some salad leaves.

EDWARD'S HANDY HINT: For ease of slicing this terrine is best made at least the day before you need it and will last in your fridge for several days.

LITTLE POTS OF PATÉ

Paté is still as popular today on both home and restaurant menus as it was in the height of its reign on restaurant menus in the seventies. I think these make a perfect addition to any party; they are really tasty and they look very quirky in this presentation. Don't rush when making this paté, the results will definitely be well worth while!

Serves 6

A little oil for cooking

5oz/150g bacon lardons

¹/₂ onion, finely chopped

2 sprigs thyme, woody stems removed

2 cloves of garlic

1lb/450g chicken livers

3 bay leaves

1 measure of brandy

4oz/110g butter, softened & cut into cubes

Topping:

4oz/110g clarified butter (see Edward's Handy Hints)

6 small sprigs of thyme

Begin by selecting the jars or pots for your pate. You can use a variety including some fancy glasses, small bowls and sterilised glass food jars.

Heat a little oil in a large wide-based frying pan and cook the bacon, onion, thyme and garlic until the onions have softened and the bacon is cooked, but not coloured.

Add the chicken livers and bay leaves.

Increase the heat and cook for about 3-4 minutes until the liver is nicely browned on the outside, but still pink and soft in the centre. It is important not to overcook the liver as it will lead to a tough paté. It will look quite unsightly at this stage, but do persevere as the end results are delicious!

Pour in the brandy, allow the alcohol to evaporate off (be careful at this stage as it may ignite and simmer for a further 2-3 minutes.

Turn off the heat and remove the bay leaves. Leave to rest for 1-2 minutes

Move the mixture to a food processor and blitz to a smooth purée.

With the food processor still running, gradually add in the softened butter and continue to blend until a relatively smooth consistency has been achieved. Season to taste.

Divide the mixture between the six glass pots or jars. Allow to cool slightly and then transfer to the fridge for at least two hours.

Remove the jars from the fridge, carefully sit a sprig of fresh thyme on top of each and then carefully cover the pate and thyme with a layer of clarified butter and return to the fridge for another 3-4 hours or preferably overnight.

Serve as required with some salad, chutney and melba toast.

EDWARD'S HANDY HINTS: The paté can be made up 2-3 days in advance so it takes another bit of stress out of your dinner party.

Clarified butter is made by separating the milk solids and water from the butter fat. Heat the butter and then allow the butter to rest for a few minutes. Through density the milk solids sink to the bottom and are left behind as the butter fat is poured into a jug for use as clarified butter.

NEW-STYLE CORONATION CHICKEN

Coronation Chicken has been around for such a long time – since the coronation of Queen Elizabeth in England 1953 in fact – and there are so many different recipes for it that I'm sure it's become nearly unrecognisable. That being said, I am particularly partial to my version of the traditional cold curried chicken dish.

Serves 6

Oven Poached Chicken:

6 chicken breasts

1 glass of white wine

1 glass of water

1 lemon, cut into wedges

Parsley stalks

Cracked black pepper

Sauce:

$1/_2$ red chilli, deseeded and finely diced

2 cloves garlic, crushed

$1/_2$ medium onion, finely chopped

1 tablespoon curry powder

1 glass white wine

2floz/50ml chicken stock

2 tablespoons mango chutney

Dash Worcestershire sauce

7floz/200ml mayonnaise

7floz/200ml natural yoghurt

Garnish:

Shredded lettuce

2oz/50g sultanas

2oz/50g ready to eat apricots, finely diced

3 stems spring onions, chopped

3oz/75g flaked almonds, lightly toasted on a dry frying pan

Fresh coriander or flat leaf parsley

OVEN POACHED CHICKEN

Preheat oven to 170C/325F/Gas Mark 3.

Place the chicken in a roasting tray and sprinkle with the cracked black pepper. Toss in the parsley stalks along with the lemon wedges and pour over the wine and the water. Cover the tray with tin foil and cook for half an hour until cooked through and firm to the touch.

Allow to chill and use as required.

SAUCE

Heat a large wide-based pan with a little oil. Add in the diced chilli, garlic and onion and sauté on a gentle heat for 2-3 minutes until just beginning to soften. Add in the curry powder and allow this to fry off a little, to release the flavours of the spices. Pour in the white wine, chicken stock and mango chutney and whisk until combined. Bring the mixture to a gentle boil and cook gently for 3-4 minutes to cook out the grainy texture of the curry powder. Transfer to a bowl and allow to cool down completely. When the mixture has cooled whisk in the mayonnaise and natural yoghurt and the Worchestershire sauce and mix well until combined.

GARNISH

Shred the cooked and cooled chicken into a large bowl and add the sultanas and apricots and mix well. Pour over the creamy curried dressing and mix to combine. Decoratively arrange the chicken on a large platter, onto a bed of shredded lettuce and garnish with the chopped spring onions, some flaked toasted almonds and flatleaf parsley.

ROAST SIRLOIN OF BEEF, TRADITIONAL GRAVY

Our home, when we were growing up, would have been quite traditional and I remember waking up on a Sunday morning to the smell of a delicious roast, be it chicken, lamb, pork or beef. I remember when it was cooked we would all argue about who got the outside slice, how soft we liked the marrowfat peas and how much room there was in our tummies for Mum's special trifle. Food for memories! And you can create wonderful memories of your own family celebrations with this delicious roast!

Serves 8-10

4lb 8oz/2kg sirloin beef

3 large carrots, cut into chunks

1 medium onion, cut into chunks

Marinade:

2 teaspoons Dijon mustard

2 large sprigs of thyme

2 tablespoons oil

4 cloves garlic, peeled

6 black peppercorns

Gravy:

2 tablespoons plain flour

$^1/_2$ glass red wine

1 pint/600ml chicken/beef stock

1 teaspoon wholegrain mustard (optional)

Scatter the chunks of carrots and onions onto the base of a deep roasting tray and place the piece of meat on top.

Preheat the oven to 200C/400F/Gas Mark 6.

Place all the ingredients for the marinade into the food processor and blitz until a chunky consistency has been achieved. Rub this all over the beef and if time allows leave this to marinade for a couple of hours or even overnight.

Place the meat in the oven and roast for 15-20 minutes per pound for medium beef. If you would like the beef more well done leave it in for an additional half an hour. After the first twenty minutes of cooking reduce the heat to 170C/325F/Gas Mark 3. Once the meat comes out of the oven allow it to rest for at least fifteen minutes prior to carving it.

While the meat is resting, begin to make the gravy.

Remove the joint of meat and the now caramelised onions and carrots from the roasting tray and place the tray on direct heat on the hob. Add in the flour and whisk until the mixture becomes dry and lumpy in consistency.

Whisk in the red wine and beef stock slowly.

Strain through a fine sieve into a clean saucepan and continue to cook for ten minutes. Add in the mustard, if using, and serve drizzled over the beef.

ASIAN CRUSTED SALMON

I love the combination of oriental flavours in this dish, and it's a perfect option as part of a buffet lunch or supper. Salmon is a popular fish in Irish homes, but sometimes it needs a helping hand flavour-wise and with this fragrant marinade and unusual nutty crust it will become a staple at your dinner parties and special family celebrations.

Serves 12

12 salmon darnes/fillets

Marinade:

2 tablespoons honey

4 floz/110 ml soy sauce

2 cloves garlic, crushed

1 inch root ginger, crushed

Crust:

6 oz/175 g cashew nuts, roughly crushed

Grated zest & juice of 1 lime

2 tablespoons coriander, chopped

$^{1}/_{2}$ red chilli, finely diced

To Serve:

Mixed salad leaves

Lime wedges

Mix together all the ingredients for the marinade in a large bowl.

Add in the salmon darnes and mix well to ensure they are completely coated.

Leave the salmon darnes to marinate for at least 30 minutes; if time allows, 2-3 hours would be even better.

Meanwhile in a small mixing bowl, mix together all the ingredients for the crust. Preheat the oven to 180C/350F/Gas Mark 4. Line two baking trays with some baking parchment. Place the salmon darnes and the marinade on the prepared baking trays, six on each, divide the nutty crust between the salmon darnes and bake in the preheated oven for 20 minutes.

Remove from the oven, allow to cool down and refrigerate overnight.

To serve, arrange some mixed lettuce leaves onto a large serving platter, arrange the chilled and crusted salmon darnes on top and garnish with the lime wedges.

EDWARD'S HANDY HINTS: This salmon is delicious served warm with a tasty noodle stir fry or some steamed green vegetables. Feel free to use this cooking method for other fish such as seabass or monkfish.

Do not leave the salmon to marinate overnight as the marinade is just too strong.

HOT AND SPICY BEEF CURRY

I simply love a curry, but it is so difficult to get a good one. This recipe is deliciously creamy and as with all curries it tastes even better on the second day. Whenever I serve a curry at home I always make it 'self service' – I just put everything (curry, rice, chutney, naan bread, yoghurt) into the middle of the table and let people help themselves. This recipe can be very easy multiplied so it's perfect for catering for larger numbers.

Serves 6

A little oil for cooking

1 ¹/₂ lb/700g stewing beef, cut into chunks

3 cloves of garlic, diced

1 red chilli, finely diced

1 medium onion, sliced very thinly

1 teaspoon tomato purée

2 tablespoons mild curry powder

1 rounded tablespoon flour

¹/₂ teaspoon turmeric

¹/₂ teaspoon ground cumin

Pinch ground ginger

7 floz/200ml pouring cream/coconut milk

1 ¹/₂ pints/800ml boiling hot beef stock

Salt & freshly-ground black pepper

10oz/300g vegetables of your choice. You can use most vegetables, I normally use mixed peppers, carrots, mushrooms, mangetout and so on.

Begin by preparing the vegetables. Preheat a medium saucepan and add a little oil – not too much, just enough to stop things from sticking.

Add the sliced beef and cook for a couple of minutes until it is sealed all over. At this stage season lightly with a little salt and pepper.

Next add in the sliced onions, diced garlic and chilli (and mixed vegetables if you are using them) and allow them to cook quite gently until they are softened and glazed with the meat juices. This stage should take about 4-5 minutes.

Now is the ideal time to add in the tomato purée and allow it to coat the meat; this will give the curry a developed taste and flavour as well as helping with the formation of colour.

Next add the curry powder together with the flour, turmeric, cumin & ginger and allow them to coat all the contents of the pot and to dry up any juices. You will get a wonderfully fragrant aroma in the kitchen at this stage! The beef stock can go in now. Allow this mixture to come to the boil then add the pouring cream or coconut milk and allow it to re-boil. I normally reduce the heat at this stage and allow the curry to cook gently for about an hour and a half. It's important to let it cook for a while to cook out the 'gritty' taste of the curry powder.

Taste and season as required. Serve the curry steaming hot with some freshly-boiled basmati rice and some naan bread – and perhaps a cool beer!

EDWARD'S HANDY HINTS: If cooking the curry in its entirety on the stove top does not suit you feel free to transfer it into a casserole dish and cook it in the oven on a moderate heat. If you would like your vegetables a little crunchier just sauté them up on a pan separately and add to the curry before serving.

RICH LAMB CASSEROLE WITH GRATIN TOPPING

This is a real winter warmer, perfect for those chilly winter days. If you are entertaining at home for a special family occasion in winter a cold buffet is not an option, but this dish would work really well and it can be happily cooking away in the oven whilst you entertain your guests.

Serves 6

1 tablespoon oil

2lb/900g stewing lamb, cut into cubes

2 medium onions, diced

3 cloves garlic, chopped

2 large carrots, cut into cubes

7oz/200g turnip, cut into cubes

8-10 button mushrooms, sliced or quartered

2 tablespoons plain flour

Tiny pinch cayenne pepper/ smoked paprika

1 1/2 pints/800ml well-flavoured chicken/beef stock

1/2 glass red wine

3-4 sprigs of fresh thyme

1 tablespoon tomato purée

1 tablespoon Worcestershire sauce

Salt & freshly-ground black pepper

Topping:

4 large potatoes, peeled and thinly sliced

1oz/25g butter, melted

Heat a large saucepan with the oil over a gentle heat and add in the diced lamb and quickly seal the meat all over. Once the meat has browned off (approx 4-5 minutes) add in the button mushrooms, onions, garlic, carrot & turnip together with a little salt and pepper. Cook for a further moment or two.

Next mix the flour with a little cayenne pepper and add this to the lamb mixture in the saucepan and use it to coat all of the lamb and vegetables with the flour. This will give a fluffy, dry coating to the contents of the saucepan. Do not worry about the flour browning off as this will just give a good colour to the sauce later on.

Gradually pour in the stock and stir continuously until the sauce begins to thicken. Add in the red wine, tomato puree, thyme sprigs and Worcestershire sauce now and allow the entire mixture to come to the boil. Once the mixture comes to the boil, reduce the heat and simmer for 1½ -2 hours until the lamb is tender. Preheat the oven to 190C/375F/Gas Mark 5.

Transfer the entire mixture to a large casserole dish and allow to cool slightly. Arrange the thinly-sliced potatoes on top of the cooled mixture in a decorative fashion. Brush with the melted butter and pop into the oven for 25-30 minutes until the potatoes are cooked through. Sprinkle with some chopped parsley.

STEAMED CHOCOLATE PUDDING CHOCOLATE AND BAILEY'S SAUCE

As children, we were thrilled when my mother made one of her best culinary hits 'Hot & Cold' – steamed chocolate pudding with vanilla ice cream. We thought at the time – and still do! – that it was culinary euphoria. This adaptation of 'Hot & Cold' is one of my favourite dessert recipes and no family occasion is complete in the Hayden household with out Mum's steamed chocolate pudding. It is a great dish to have cooked in advance, which is an added bonus and you can just heat it up when required.

Serves 6

Pudding

4oz/110g butter, softened

4oz/110g caster sugar

4 eggs

5oz/150g plain flour

1 teaspoon baking powder

1oz/25g cocoa powder

Chocolate and Bailey's Sauce

8floz/225ml pouring cream

4oz/110g dark chocolate, chopped

1 measure of Baileys (optional)

Lightly grease a 2lb/900g pudding basin with some melted butter.

In a large mixing bowl, cream the butter and sugar together until light and fluffy. This should take 5-6 minutes. Add in the eggs and mix completely.

Sieve the plain flour with the baking powder and cocoa powder, then add these to the creamy mixture in the bowl and stir until completely smooth.

Pour into the prepared pudding basin, cover the top of the basin with tinfoil and then secure the lid. Bring a large saucepan of water to the boil and sit the pudding basin into the pot, ensuring that that the water comes no more than halfway up the side of the basin.

Simmer for 1½-1¾ hours, keeping an eye on the pot while it's steaming to make sure that the water does evaporate. Top up with additional water as required. When the pudding is cooked (a skewer inserted in the centre will come out clean), invert it onto a serving platter and set aside.

TO MAKE THE SAUCE

Put the cream into a small saucepan and bring to a rapid boil. Pour the boiled cream onto the chopped chocolate and mix well. Whisk in the Bailey's into the sauce and pour the sauce generously over the steamed pudding.

EDWARD'S HANDY HINT: Feel free to add in some rum-soaked raisins (approx 4oz/110g) to the pudding mixture before steaming for added flavour.

EDWARD'S SPECIAL RASPBERRY MERINGUE CAKE

This is a recipe that I have tried and experimented with in several different ways in an attempt to get it perfect. This cake is irresistibly delicious – a real 'special occasion' cake – and will wow your family and friends when it graces your table.

Serves 8-10

Cake Mixture:

8oz/225g butter, softened

8oz/225g sugar

4 large eggs

A little milk (optional)

6oz/175g self-raising flour

2oz/50g ground almonds

5oz/150g fresh/frozen raspberries

Meringue Topping:

3 egg whites

6oz/175g caster sugar

1oz/25g flaked almonds

Garnish:

2 tablespoons raspberry jam

Fresh raspberries

Mint leaves

1oz/25g toasted flaked almonds

9floz/250ml whipped cream

Chocolate shavings

Preheat the oven to 170C/325F/Gas Mark 3.

Grease a 9inch/23cm springform tin and line the base and sides of it with parchment paper.

In a large mixing bowl or electric mixer cream the butter and the sugar together until light and fluffy. Add in the eggs, then sieve together the flour and ground almonds and add these to the mixture also. Mix well until a creamy consistency has been achieved, adding a little milk if necessary to loosen the consistency. Gently fold in the raspberries and then pour the mixture into the prepared cake tin. Put into the oven and cook for forty minutes.

Meanwhile make the meringue: whisk together the egg whites with an electric mixer until very stiff and then gradually add in the caster sugar and continue to whisk on full speed until the mixture is thick and glossy.

Remove the cake from the oven; it will still be slightly undercooked. Very quickly pile the meringue on top of the sponge, spreading it over the top of the cake. Sprinkle with the flaked almonds and return to the oven immediately.

Reduce the oven temperature to 150C/300f/Gas Mark 2 and continue to cook the cake for a further 25-30 minutes.

Remove the cake from the oven and allow it to cool completely in the tin, preferably overnight.

ASSEMBLY

Remove the cake from the tin, peel off the parchment paper and carefully split the sponge horizontally in two equal pieces. Transfer the bottom part of the sponge to a cake stand/serving platter and spread with the raspberry jam. Carefully place the remaining piece on top, to return the cake to its original structure.

Pile the whipped cream on the top and then arrange some fresh raspberries on top. Decorate with some mint leaves, toasted flaked almonds and some chocolate shavings.

EDWARD'S HANDY HINT: If you wish you can change the flavour of this cake by varying the fruits. Sometimes I spread some whipped cream in the centre of the cake for added indulgence.

BEST-EVER TIRAMISU

There are so many different versions of tiramisu out there, but this simple version is still my favourite and can be prepared in minutes.

Serves 6

Approximately 18-24 boudoir biscuits

14oz/400g mascarpone cheese

7floz/200ml cream, whipped

2 cups strong black coffee

3 tablespoons brandy/amaretto

Cocoa powder, to garnish

Place the coffee and alcohol into a flat dish.

Select six serving glasses. Mix together the mascarpone cheese and the whipped cream and add in three tablespoons of the coffee mixture.

Dip each biscuit into the coffee mixture and then immediately layer them decoratively in the serving glasses, placing some of the creamy mixture in between each layer. Finish with a layer of the creamy filling and then dust liberally with cocoa powder just before serving.

EDWARD'S HANDY HINT: It's best to leave them to rest for an hour or two before serving.

You could double this mixture and build it in a flat baking dish as a large dessert option.

You could also add a tablespoon of icing sugar to the cheese for added sweetness.

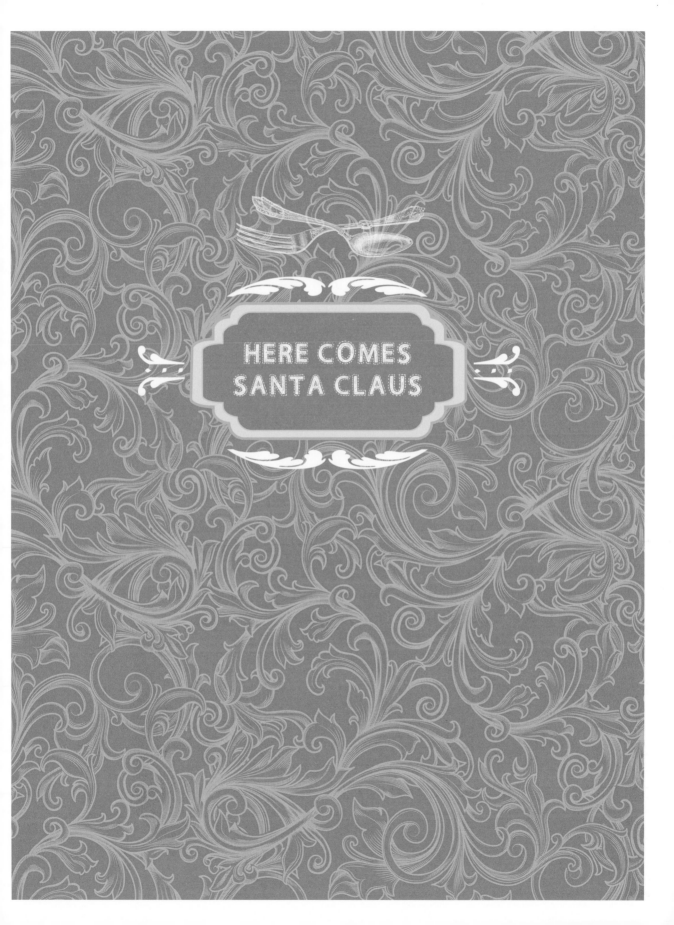

HERE COMES
SANTA CLAUS

EDWARD'S CHRISTMAS CANAPÉS – FIVE WAYS TO NIBBLE THROUGH CHRISTMAS

1. PAN-SEARED SCALLOPS, LEMON AND SUNDRIED TOMATO BUTTER

Serves 12

Lemon & Sundried Tomato Butter:

3oz/75g butter

2 tablespoons sundried tomatoes, chopped

1 tablespoon parsley, chopped

Zest of 1 lemon, grated

Pan-Seared Scallops:

A little oil for cooking

12 large scallops

1oz/25g butter

Salt & freshly-ground black pepper

To serve:

12 bread croutons

A handful of chopped parsley

Scallops are a wonderfully flavoursome option to have when planning a party and the citrus flavour of the butter is a great addition to this dish.

Melt the butter in a small saucepan. Add in the grated lemon zest, sundried tomatoes and chopped parsley and mix well. Store in a warm place until required; I normally store it beside the cooker to keep the butter nice and soft.

PAN-SEARED SCALLOPS

Heat a large pan with a little oil.

Lay the scallops out flat on a plate or chopping board.

Season the scallops with a little salt and black pepper.

Toss them into the pan and cook for about a minute on either side on a very hot pan until golden brown. Add in the butter to get a nice glaze.

Allow to sit for a moment and then serve.

ASSEMBLY

Sit each pan-seared scallop on a toasted crouton of bread and garnish with a little fresh parsley.

Serve the lemon & sundried tomato butter to the side.

• •

2. MINI BRUSCHETTA WITH RED ONION MARMALADE AND BLUE CHEESE

Serves 20

Red Onion Marmalade:

4 medium red onions, peeled and thinly sliced.

3oz/75g brown sugar

3 tablespoons red wine

3 tablespoons red wine vinegar

1 teaspoon of oil

The combinations of flavours are superb in this dish and are well worth the effort involved.

In a large pot, heat the onions and the oil over a high heat. Keep moving the onions around to prevent them from sticking. As the onions begin to colour and soften (after about three minutes) add in the brown sugar and continue to stir; the sugar will begin to soften and will coat all the onions. Allow the softened sugar to come to the boil gently, then add the red wine and the red wine vinegar.

Allow the mixture to come to the boil and then simmer for about 10-15 minutes or until all of the liquid has evaporated off. Keep stirring occasionally to prevent anything sticking to the base of the pot. Transfer to clean sterilized jars and store in the fridge for up to 4 weeks. Preheat the oven to 190C/375F/Gas Mark 5.

Brush the sliced bread with a little oil and place onto a flat baking tray and transfer to the pre-heated oven. Cook for 10-12 minutes until they are crisp. Allow to cool down.

Bruschetta Topping:

Red onion marmalade

2 tablespoons crème fraiche

10 cherry tomatoes, halved

4oz/110g blue cheese

Fresh rocket

Croutons:

2 medium baguettes cut into slices approx 1 inch thick

3 tablespoons oil

ASSEMBLY

Spread some of the crème fraiche on top of each crouton. Arrange a spoon of the red onion marmalade on top of each along with a half a cherry tomato. Crumble some blue cheese on top of each and then top with some fresh rocket leaves.

EDWARD'S HANDY HINTS: To sterilize the jars wash them out with boiling water and then place in a warm oven (130C/250F/Gas Mark $\frac{1}{2}$)for approximately 15-20 minutes until completely dry. Wash the lids in boiling water and allow to dry in a warm place

- -

3. SEAFOOD VOL-AU-VENTS

I think Christmas is a great time to bring back the classics – this is my take on a classic and very popular dish.

Preheat the oven to 190C/375F/Gas Mark 5.

Arrange the vol-au-vent cases onto a flat baking tray. Brush the edges with the egg wash and cook according to the packet instructions until they are golden brown. The vol-au-vents are best cooked in advance and filled only when required. The heat of the seafood sauce will sufficiently reheat the pastry case.

Serves 18

1 pack medium-sized vol-au-vent cases

Egg wash (1 egg mixed with 1 tablespoon milk)

Seafood Filling:

1oz/25g butter

1 leek, thinly sliced

6-8 button mushrooms, thinly sliced

2 cloves of garlic, crushed

1 tablespoon plain flour

$\frac{1}{2}$ glass white wine

8floz/225ml fish stock

4floz/110ml pouring cream

1lb/450g selection of fish (include cod, salmon, smoked fish etc)

Salt & freshly-ground black pepper

1 tablespoon parsley, freshly-chopped

SEAFOOD FILLING

Sauté the leeks and mushrooms in the butter, along with the crushed garlic cloves until they are glazed, but without colour. Sprinkle in the plain flour and use it to coat all of the vegetables and dry up all the juices.

Add in white wine and fish stock together with cream and allow the mixture to come to a gentle boil. Reduce the heat at this stage and simmer for 10-12 minutes.

At this stage the vegetables will have softened and you can add in the fish. Try not to stir the mix too much as this will cause the fish to break up.

Cook, very gently, for 5-6 minutes just until the fish is cooked.

Season lightly and divide between the cooked vol-au-vent cases and sprinkle with some freshly-chopped parsley.

Makes 24

1 1/2 lb/700g lean minced beef
2 tablespoons cranberry sauce
1 medium onion, diced
3 sticks celery, finely diced
2oz/50g fine white
breadcrumbs
1 egg
1oz/25g grated cheese
(parmesan, cheddar, blue
cheese etc)
1/2 teaspoon ground cinnamon
1 tablespoon parsley, freshly
chopped

4. CRANBERRY AND CINNAMON MEAT BALLS

The quintessential festive flavours of cinnamon and cranberry go down a treat in this dish!

Preheat the oven to 180C/350F/Gas Mark 4.

Place the meat into a large bowl. Add the cranberry sauce, diced onion & celery, egg and breadcrumbs together with the grated cheese, cinnamon and chopped parsley. Mix thoroughly until combined and then divide the mixture into approximately 24 small pieces and then roll each piece into medium sized meatballs. Place the meatballs onto a baking tray lined with parchment paper and pop into the preheated oven for 15-20 minutes to allow them to cook, turning occasionally as they cook. When cooked the meatballs should be firm to the touch.

Thread the meatballs onto skewers and serve immediately.

• •

Makes 24

Mini Wholemeal Scones
8oz/225g extra coarse
wholemeal flour
8oz/225g self-raising flour
1 rounded teaspoon baking
powder
Pinch salt
2oz/50g brown sugar
2oz/50g hard butter
1 egg
7floz/200ml buttermilk (approx)
2 tablespoons porridge oats
Egg wash (1 egg mixed with 1
tablespoon milk)

Makes 24

Thai-Style Crab Cocktail:
1lb/450g fresh white crabmeat
3 tablespoons crème fraiche
2 tablespoons sweet chilli sauce
Pinch cayenne pepper
Approximately 4oz/110g
sundried tomatoes
Large handful of rocket leaves

5. THAI-STYLE CRAB COCKTAIL ON MINI WHOLEMEAL SCONES

MINI WHOLEMEAL SCONES

Preheat the oven to 190C/375F/Gas Mark 5.

Sieve the self raising flour and baking powder into the wholemeal flour, then stir in the sugar and the salt. Rub the butter in with your fingertips until it resembles rough breadcrumbs. Add the egg and mix well and then carefully pour in the buttermilk until the mixture comes together, adding a little extra buttermilk if required. Knead the mixture on a lightly floured work surface, flatten out slightly and then using a small scone cutter, cut the dough into approximately 12-15 pieces. Brush the tops of the scones lightly with egg wash and place on a greased tray. Sprinkle the porridge oats over the top and bake for 18-20 minutes.

THAI-STYLE CRAB COCKTAIL

While the scones are baking, mix together the crème fraiche and sweet chilli sauce. Once the scones are baked and have had time to cool down, split each one in half, butter each half and arrange on a large serving platter Place some rocket leaves on top of each scone. Pick through the crab meat to ensure that all traces of shell have been removed and then divide it between the scones. Spoon a little of the sweet chilli crème fraiche on top of each and then garnish with a little sun dried tomato.

Decorate, sparingly, with a little dusting of cayenne pepper.

TRADITIONAL ROAST TURKEY BREAST WITH CRANBERRY GRAVY

For those who don't want to be looking at leftover turkey for the whole Christmas period, I have chosen to cook just a breast of turkey. This is also good for those who only like white meat. You could keep this recipe to hand also for your home entertaining requirements as it can be quite nice to served carved turkey as part of a home buffet.

Serves 6

1 large breast of turkey
(approx 5-6lb weight)
2 carrots, diced
1 large onion, diced
4-6 cloves garlic
1oz/25g butter
4-5 rashers of bacon
Salt & freshly-ground black
pepper
3-4 sprigs of thyme
A little oil, for drizzling

Roast Gravy:
1 tablespoon plain flour
1 glass red wine
18floz/500ml chicken stock
4oz/110g fresh/frozen
cranberries

Preheat the oven to 190C/375F/Gas Mark 5.

Select a large roasting tray and scatter the carrots, onion, garlic cloves and sprigs of thyme over the roasting tray.

Next, soften the butter slightly and carefully manoeuvre your hand underneath the skin of the turkey and slide in the softened butter. Massage this into the breast of the turkey to add succulence. Season with a little salt and pepper and carefully lay the rashers of bacon on top of the turkey. Place the prepared turkey breast on top of the herbs and vegetables on the tray.

Drizzle with a tiny amount of oil (to stop the butter from burning) and transfer to the preheated oven. After the first hour, reduce the heat of the oven to 170C/325F/Gas Mark 3 and cook for a further hour or until a skewer inserted in the meat causes the juices to run clear. At this stage the meat should also be soft and tender and not feel at all hard when you're pushing in the skewer. Remove from the oven, cover tightly with tin foil and allow to rest for twenty minutes before carving.

Remove the vegetables form the roasting tray and place the tray containing the flavoursome meat juices on the stove top then whisk the plain flour into the juices. Continue to whisk on a medium heat the stove top until the flour is browned. Pour in the glass of red wine and the stock and whisk until fully incorporated. Sieve the gravy into a clean saucepan, add the cranberries and boil for about ten minutes, until you have achieved a nice coating sauce.

EDWARD'S HANDY HINTS: If you wish to cook a full turkey, you could stuff it with the apple, cranberry and sausage-meat stuffing (see p177 – follow the terrine recipe until just before the mixture goes into the loaf tin) and cook for twenty minutes per lb/450g and then 20 minutes more.

APPLE, CRANBERRY AND SAUSAGE-MEAT STUFFING

This is a nice alternative to stuffing the entire bird in that you actually end up with a loaf of stuffing. The bacon lends great flavour to the stuffing and because of the cooked sausage meat it cuts quite well after it has been sufficiently rested. Play around with the flavourings to find your preferred combination.

Serves 6

3oz/75g butter

1 small onion, diced

3oz/75g fresh cranberries

4 tablespoons mixed herbs, parsley, sage, thyme, finely chopped

1 cooking apple, grated or finely chopped

7oz/200g fresh white breadcrumbs

12oz/350g sausage meat (approx 10-12 sausages)

14-16 rashers of streaky bacon, approx

Heat the butter in a medium saucepan and gently fry the diced onion for 4–5 minutes until it has softened, but yet not coloured. Add in the cranberries and the chopped mixed herbs and immediately turn off the heat. Allow this mixture to cool completely before adding it to the sausage meat mixture.

Add this 'buttery onion' mixture to a large mixing bowl and add in the grated apple, breadcrumbs and sausage meat. Season with salt and pepper.

Meanwhile preheat the oven to 180C/350F/Gas Mark 4.

Select a 2lb/900g loaf tin and line it with the rashers of streaky bacon, making sure that there is an overhang of the bacon at both sides; you'll use this to close in and encase the terrine at a later stage. Push the stuffing into the bacon-lined loaf tin and then encase the stuffing with the bacon overhang. Bake in the oven for 1¼ hours and then check to make sure it is cooked by inserting a knife into the centre. The juices should be clear and the knife should feel hot to the touch. Allow the stuffing terrine to rest for at least half an hour before serving. Slice and serve alongside the moist turkey.

ALTERNATIVE FLAVOURS

Apricot & hazelnut

Apple & walnut

SUGGESTED AMOUNTS

6 apricots & 3oz/75g crushed hazelnuts

1 grated cooking apple & 3oz/75g chopped walnuts

WHOLE ROAST DUCK WITH APRICOT AND HAZELNUT STUFFING

Sometimes people are looking for an alternative to the traditional Christmas turkey and this could be it. A friend of mine rears her own ducks and turkeys each year and they are truly superb. This would also make a delicious option as a main course for a pre-Christmas dinner party.

Serves 4

1 large oven-ready duck

Stuffing:

3oz/75g butter

$\frac{1}{2}$ medium onion, diced

2 tablespoons mixed herbs, parsley, thyme, rosemary, chives, finely chopped

6oz/175g breadcrumbs

10 diced dried apricots, roughly chopped

2oz/50g hazelnuts, skinned

Salt & freshly-ground black pepper

Preheat the oven to 200C/400F/Gas Mark 6.

To make the stuffing, melt the butter in a medium saucepan, add the onion and then sweat them in the butter over a low heat for 3-4 minutes. At this stage add the freshly-chopped mixed herbs. Next mix in the fresh white breadcrumbs and stir in the apricots and hazelnuts. Season the mixture with a little salt and pepper and allow to cool completely. Line the cavity of the duck with parchment paper and fill with the flavoured stuffing. Place into a dry roasting tray and roast for 1¼ -1½ hours until it is golden brown and cooked through.

Serve with some crispy roasted potatoes and green vegetables.

EDWARD'S HANDY HINTS: Soaking some cranberries in port and adding them to the stuffing makes a tremendous difference and it gives a great flavour. Using leftover mashed potatoes in place of the breadcrumbs in the stuffing is not only a great way of using up the potato, but also gives a varied consistency to the stuffing and is perfect for those looking for a gluten-free option.

VEGETARIAN MOUSSAKA

At Christmas, when family and friends come round for Christmas dinner it's nice to make an extra special effort with your culinary endeavours. If you have vegetarian guests coming and you are not that familiar with vegetarian cooking then this simple and tasty dish is just the recipe for you. I think that both the cook and the guest will be happy with the results.

Serves 6

3 large aubergines, cut into slices (approx 20 slices)
7oz/200g dried green lentils
A little oil for cooking
1 pint/600ml vegetable stock
1 red onion, thinly sliced
2 cloves of garlic
8-10 button mushrooms, sliced
14oz/400g can chickpeas, rinsed
14oz/400g tinned chopped tomatoes
1 teaspoon tomato purée
$\frac{1}{2}$ teaspoon of dried mixed herbs
3 $\frac{1}{2}$ floz/100ml cold water
Salt & freshly-ground black pepper

Topping:
10 floz/300ml natural yoghurt
3 floz/75ml milk
2 large eggs
Salt & freshly ground black pepper
3oz/75g cheddar or mozzarella cheese

Preheat the oven to 180C/350F/Gas Mark 4.

Put the lentils in a large saucepan with the vegetable stock and bring them to the boil and then simmer for twenty minutes until tender. Drain and keep warm.

Meanwhile, heat some oil in a saucepan and cook the red onion, mushroom and garlic until soft and tender.

Stir in the cooked lentils, chickpeas, chopped tomatoes, purée, herbs and water. Bring to the boil and simmer for ten minutes, stirring occasionally.

Pan-fry the aubergine slices until brown on either side.

Lightly grease a 9 inch/23 cm square ovenproof baking dish.

Season the lentil mixture and layer up the aubergines and the lentil mixture much like a lasagne, starting and finishing with aubergine.

For the topping beat the yoghurt, milk, eggs and seasoning together.

Pour over the vegetable mixture and then sprinkle the cheese over the top

Bake in the preheated oven for forty-five minutes.

Serve with a large salad or crusty bread.

DUNDEE CAKE

Dundee cake is a famous Scottish fruit cake. If you don't like a very rich and moist Christmas cake this makes for a wonderful option as it is lighter and crumblier in consistency. For as long as I can remember my mother baked one of these every Christmas as well as the traditional rich iced Christmas cake.

Serves 6

8oz/225g butter

8oz/225g demerara sugar

5 large eggs

10oz/300g plain flour

¹/₂ teaspoon bread soda

1 teaspoon mixed spice

8oz/225g sultanas

8oz/225g currants

4oz/110g mixed peel

2oz/50g cherries

6oz/175g blanched almonds, whole

Pinch of salt

Glaze:

1 tablespoon apricot jam

2 tablespoons water

Preheat the oven to 150C/300F/Gas Mark 2.

Grease an 8inch/20cm tin and line it with baking parchment, then line the outside of the tin with some brown paper, tightly secured in place with string.

In a large electric mixer cream the butter and sugar until light and fluffy. Whisk the eggs and add them to the buttery mixture. Sieve in the flour, mixed spice, salt and bread soda at this stage and stir thoroughly until combined. Next add in the sultanas, currants, cherries and mixed peel and ensure that they too are well incorporated into the mixture. Transfer into the prepared tin, levelling the surface of the cake with a spoon. Neatly arrange the blanched almonds in a circular pattern over the top of the cake and then transfer to the preheated oven for 2 ½ hours or until a skewer inserted in the centre comes out clean.

Just before the cake is due to come out of the oven, put the apricot jam into a small saucepan with the water and mix together over a medium heat until the mixture comes to the boil and then brush this over the surface of the cake when it comes out of the oven. Allow the cake to cool in its tin and then carefully transfer onto a large serving platter.

This will keep fresh in an airtight container for up to two weeks.

EDWARD'S HANDY HINT: For added flavour, you could pour some whiskey or brandy over the cake.

WHITE CHOCOLATE AND RASPBERRY TRIFLE

Trifle is one of those desserts that each family has their own unique recipe for and a recipe which they tend, year on year, not to deviate from. This particular recipe, take it from me, will have your family and friends begging for trifle for breakfast. There are a couple of different elements to this recipe but it is definitely well worth the effort.

Serves 6

Swiss Roll:

4 eggs

4oz/110g caster sugar

4oz/110g self-raising flour

2 tablespoons raspberry jam

White Chocolate Custard:

$\frac{1}{2}$ pint/300ml milk

$\frac{1}{2}$ pint/300ml cream

6 egg yolks

3oz/75g sugar

5oz/150g white chocolate, cut into chunks

2 teaspoons cornflour

Decoration:

6oz/175g fresh/frozen raspberries

9floz/250ml freshly whipped cream

2oz/50g toasted flaked almonds

Preheat the oven to 180C/350F/Gas Mark 4.

Grease and line an oblong (13 x 9 inch/32 x 22cm) tin with parchment paper. First make the Swiss roll; in a mixing bowl beat the eggs with the sugar for about 4-5 minutes. It should become quite stiff, yet light and aerated.

Sieve the flour into the mix and using a spoon gently fold into the egg and sugar mix. Transfer into the prepared tin and bake in the preheated oven for 18-20 minutes until the sponge has turned golden in colour. Allow the sponge to cool a little on a wire tray. Once the sponge has cooled, place a clean tea towel onto the work surface and invert the sponge onto it, taking care to remove all the parchment paper. Using a rolling pin, roll it over the sponge to flatten it and then spread with the raspberry jam. Holding the corners of the tea towel closest to your body, carefully roll the Swiss roll – by pushing it away from you – up from the longest side rather than from the shortest and then slice into thin slices.

Keep back three slices of sponge, then arrange the rest of the sponge slices all the way around a large glass presentation bowl, ensuring it is lined all the way round. Scatter in ¾ of the raspberries. Next, make the custard. Put the milk and cream in a large saucepan and allow them to come to the boil. In a separate bowl, beat the white chocolate, egg yolks, sugar and cornflour together. Pour the boiled milk and cream mixture onto the egg and chocolate mixture and mix well. Return the custard to the saucepan and continue to cook, whisking continuously over a low heat, until it reaches a thick, coating consistency. Pour the white chocolate custard into the sponge-lined bowl. Push the three extra slices of sponge into the custard at this stage to fill the gap in the middle of the bowl and sit a piece of cling film directly on top of the custard to prevent a skin forming. Allow to chill in the fridge overnight. To decorate remove the layer of cling film and pile the whipped cream onto the custard and then scatter the remaining raspberries on top. Scatter the toasted flaked almonds over the top and serve immediately.

EDWARD'S HANDY HINT: Feel free to make a Black Forest trifle by adding some cocoa powder to the flour when making the Swiss roll and using fresh or tinned black cherries instead of raspberries.

TRADITIONAL MINCEMEAT

The aroma of festive baking is a memory from my childhood that will always stay with me. Now years later when I find myself emulating my mother's annual tasks it is my delight to fill our home with these most fragrant aromas. Whilst you can buy commercial mincemeat very readily nowadays there is nothing to compare to the homemade variety.

Makes approx 4 jars

2 medium cooking apples
8oz/225g brown sugar
5oz/150g butter
Zest & juice 2 oranges
4oz/110g mixed peel
2 tablespoons orange
marmalade
5oz/150g currants
10oz/300g raisins
5oz/150g sultanas
2floz/50ml Irish whiskey

Chop the apples into small pieces and add to a medium saucepan with the butter and the sugar and cook gently for 3-4 minutes. Next add all the other ingredients and continue to cook for approximately 10-15 minutes (the liquid should have come to the boil at this stage). Transfer the mixture to sterilised jars and leave to rest for a couple of weeks before using.

EDWARD'S HANDY HINT: This recipe will makes about four jars of mincemeat. The flavour develops greatly over time so the longer you can have this made before Christmas, the better!

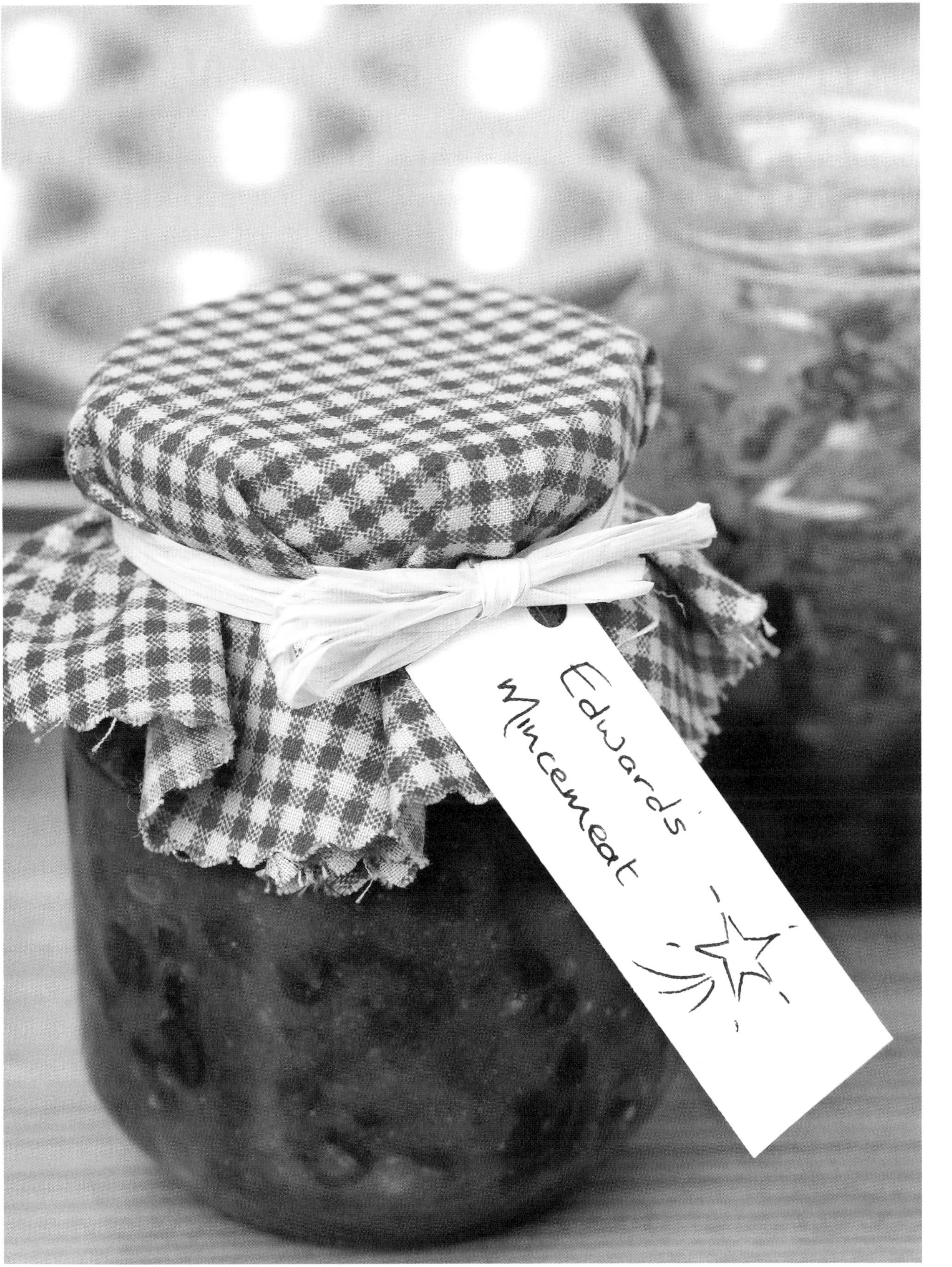
Edwards
Mincemeat

FESTIVE MINCE PIE CRUMBLES

Christmas would not be Christmas without some delicious mince pies. Feel free to buy the mincemeat if you wish – I have made my own which is well worth the effort.
If you follow my simple mincemeat recipe, you should have enough mincemeat to see you through the festive season!

Makes 12

Sweet Pastry:

10oz/300g plain flour

5oz/150g caster sugar

5oz/150g butter

1 egg

Crumble Topping:

4oz/110g plain flour

1/2 teaspoon ground cinnamon

2oz/50g brown sugar

3oz/75g butter, cut into cubes

Additional Ingredients:

1 jar of good quality mincemeat
(see p184)

6floz/175ml whipped cream

1 tablespoon Irish whiskey

SWEET PASTRY

Sieve the flour into a large mixing bowl. Add in the sugar and butter and using your fingertips rub in the butter. Lightly beat the egg and add it to the dry ingredients. Mix together until combined.
Knead on a lightly-floured work surface for a moment or two and then wrap tightly in cling film and refrigerate until required.

CRUMBLE TOPPING

Sieve the flour and cinnamon into a large mixing bowl and add the sugar. Add in the butter and using the tips of your fingers rub the mixture together until it resembles fine breadcrumbs.

ASSEMBLY

Preheat the oven to 180C/350F/Gas Mark 4.
Grease your tin (I would suggest using either a twelve-cup bun tray or a twelve-cup mini muffin tray). Roll out the chilled pastry on a lightly-floured work surface. Cut out discs of sweet pastry and use them to line your chosen bun or muffin tray. Spoon some of the mincemeat into each of the pastry line cups and then sprinkle with some of the crumble topping. Bake for 15-18 minutes.
It's delicious served with freshly-whipped Irish whiskey cream (just add a small amount of whiskey to the cream once it's whipped).

EDWARD'S HANDY HINTS:
If you prefer, you can use a pastry disc on top of the mince pie instead of the crumble topping.
You can make the pastry in advance and store in the fridge or freezer until required for a later batch of mince pies.

CHOCOLATE AND HAZELNUT BISCOTTI

Biscotti are Italian twice-baked biscuits. They are quite dry and crispy and are a perfect accompaniment to dunk into coffee, crème brulées, mousses or pannacottas. Again these make a very tasty edible Christmas gift and look very attractive packaged in a jar tied with ribbon.

Makes 18

6oz/175g plain flour

1 tablespoon cocoa

1 rounded teaspoon baking powder

4oz/110g brown sugar

2 eggs, beaten together

3oz/75g hazelnuts, skinned and lightly broken

Preheat the oven to 180C/350F/Gas Mark 4.

Place flour, baking powder, cocoa powder and brown sugar in a large bowl or mixer. Add in the hazelnuts and mix well.

Mix in the beaten eggs until a dough-like consistency has been achieved; you may not need all the eggs so add them carefully.

Divide the dough in two, roughly roll into two ciabatta shapes and flatten them slightly. Bake on the greased baking tray for twenty minutes.

Remove from the oven and allow to cool slightly, then, with a sharp knife, cut them into fingers or strips and return to the baking tray and the oven and cook for 10-12 minutes and then turn them over and cook for a further ten minutes until they are browned and firm to the touch. Allow the biscotti to cool on the tin as they will firm up further as they cool, giving the desired 'crunch' effect.

EDWARD'S HANDY HINTS: Add a few mixed chocolate chips to the biscuit mix if you'd like an extra chocolate fix.

In an airtight container the biscuits last for approximately two weeks.

If the eggs do not fully bring the mixture together add a small amount of cold water.

INDEX

A

Almonds: Lemon and Almond Cake, 27
Apple
  Apple, Celery & Walnut with Natural
    Yoghurt, 76
  Edward's Apple and Rhubarb Crumble
    Cake, 142
  Apple and Walnut Stuffing, 177
  Apple, Cranberry and Sausage-meat
    Stuffing, 177
Apricots
  Moroccan Couscous, 72
  New Style Coronation Chicken, 154
  Pork and Chicken Terrine, 151
  Whole Roast Duck with Apricot and
    Hazelnut Stuffing, 178
Asian Crusted Salmon, 157
Aubergines: Vegetarian Moussaka, 179
Avocado
  Guacamole with Home-Baked Spiced
    Tortilla Chips, 106

B

Baked Ginger Pudding, Cinnamon-
  Roasted Pears with Butterscotch
  Sauce, 138
Baked Lemon Sole with Salsa Verde, 137
Baking, Sweet
  Birthday Cake, 51
  Chocolate Chip Cookies, 36
  Chocolate Marble Cake, 31
  Chocolate Truffle Cake, 141
  Dundee Cake, 180
  Edward's Apple and Rhubarb Crumble
    Cake, 142
  Edward's Chocolate Éclairs, 32
  Edward's Special Raspberry Meringue
    Cake, 165
  Festive Mince Pie Crumbles, 187
  Glazed Fruit Tart, 40
  Iced Cupcakes, 28
  Lemon and Almond Cake, 27
  Lemon Drizzle Slices, 39
  Spiced Hot Cross Buns with Orange
    Cinnamon Glaze, 24
  Steamed Chocolate Pudding, Choco-
    late and Bailey's Sauce, 162
  Sugar-Crusted Cherry Scones, 35
Baking, Savoury
  Edward's Multiseed Brown Bread, 17
  Pesto and Sundried Tomato Bread, 146
  Thai-Style Crab Cocktail on Mini
    Wholemeal Scones, 174
  White Soda Scones with Cheese and
    Thyme, 124
Basil Mayonnaise, 59
Beef, Fillet
  Beef Stroganoff, 108
  Crispy Beef Spring Rolls, 115
  Fillet of Beef with Sautéd Spinach and
    Mushroom with Black Pepper Sauce,
    133

Beef, Minced
  Brunch-Style Burger, 10
  Spaghetti Bolognaise, 48
  Cranberry and Cinnamon Meatballs,
    174
Beef, Sirloin
  Beef and Vegetable Noodle Stir
    Fry, 88
  Roast Sirloin Beef, Traditional
    Gravy, 155
Beef, Steak
  Garlic and Rosemary Scented Steaks,
    57
  Mixed Grill Skewers, 13
Beef, Stewing
  Hot and Spicy Beef Curry, 158
  Hungarian Beef Goulash, 85
  Beef Stroganoff, 108
Best-Ever Tiramisu, 166
Beef and Vegetable Noodle Stir Fry, 88
Birthday Cake, 51
Black Pepper Cream Sauce, 133
Braised Chicken with Smoked Bacon
  Cream, 91
Brunch-Style Burger, 10
Butter Icing, 28
Butternut Squash: Spiced Winter
  Vegetable Soup, 148
Butterscotch Sauce, 138

C

Chickpeas: Spiced Chickpea Broth, 96
Carrot
  Roasted Carrot and Ginger Soup, 99
  Spiced Winter Vegetable Soup, 148
Cashew Nuts
  Asian Crusted Salmon, 157
  Beef and Vegetable Noodle Stirfry, 88
  Crispy Pork Salad with Cashew Nuts
    and Sweet Potato Crisps, 82
  Sweet Chilli Noodle Salad, 68
Chargrilled Vegetable Bruschetta with
  Basil Mayonnaise, 59
Cheese, Blue
  Brunch Style Burger, 10
  Cranberry and Cinnamon
    Meatballs, 174
  Mini Bruschetta with Red Onion Mar-
    malade and Blue Cheese, 170
Cheese, Brie: Muffuletta, 21
Cheese, Cheddar
  Pitta Pizzas, 118
  Quiche in a Tin, 121
  Spicy Chicken Quesadillas, 114
  Vegetarian Moussaka, 179
  White Soda Scones with Cheese and
    Thyme, 124
Chicken Breast
  Braised Chicken with Smoked Bacon
    Cream, 91
  Chicken Breasts with Chilli Yoghurt
    Marinade, 64
  Mixed Grill Skewers, 13
  New Style Coronation Chicken, 154
  Pork and Chicken Terrine, 151

Sesame Chicken Goujons, 47
Chicken, Cooked: Spicy Chicken
  Quesadillas, 114
Chicken Drumsticks: Sweet and Sticky
  Chicken Drumsticks, 44
Chicken Livers: Little Pots of Paté, 152
Chicken on the Bone: Italian Baked
  Chicken, 95
Chicken, Whole: Whole Roasted Chicken,
  Lemon, Courgette and Pine Nut Stuff-
  ing, 92
Chilli Oil, 79
Chocolate,
  Chocolate and Hazelnut Terrine, 110
  Chocolate Marble Cake, 31
  Chocolate Truffle Cake, 141
  Edward's Chocolate Éclairs, 32
  Steamed Chocolate Pudding, Choco-
    late and Baileys Sauce, 162
  White Chocolate and Raspberry Trifle,
    183
Chocolate and Baileys Sauce, 162
Chocolate and Hazelnut Biscotti, 188
Chocolate and Hazelnut Terrine, 110
Chocolate Chip Cookies, 36
Chocolate Ganache, 32
Chocolate Marble Cake, 31
Chocolate Sponge, 141
Chocolate Truffle Cake, 141
Chocolate Truffles, 141
Chorizo: Edward's Tortilla Espanola with
  Chorizo, 18
Cinnamon Roasted Pears, 138
Clarifed Butter, 152
Cocktail Sausages: Mixed Grill
  Skewers, 13
Couscous, Moroccan, 72
Courgettes
  Chargrilled Vegetable Bruschetta with
    Basil Mayonnaise, 59
  Italian Baked Chicken, 95
  Mediterranean Vegetable Stack, 149
  Moroccan Couscous, 72
  Muffuletta, 21
  Quiche in a Tin, 121
  Spiced Indian Pakoras, 84
  Whole Roasted Chicken, Lemon, Cour-
    gette and Pine Nut Stuffing, 92
Crab Meat
  Spaghetti with Crab Meat and Chilli,
    129
  Thai-Style Crab Cocktail on Mini
    Wholemeal Scones, 174
Cranberries
  Apple, Cranberry and Sausage-Meat
    Stuffing, 177
  Traditional Roast Turkey Breast with
    Cranberry Gravy, 176
Cranberry and Cinnamon Meatballs, 174
Cranberry Sauce: Cranberry and
  Cinnamon Meatballs, 174
Creamy Potato, Leek and Thyme
  Soup, 127
Crisper than Crisp Potato Wedges, 117

Crispy Beef Spring Rolls, 115
Crispy Pork Salad with Cashew Nuts
  and Sweet Potato Crisps, 82
Crock of Mussels in a White Wine
  and Cream Broth, 128
Crumble Topping, 187
Crusted Hake with Crunchy Pine Nut
Topping, 130
D
Dressings
  Mustard Seed Dressing, 79
  Rosemary and Balsamic Infusion, 79
  Summer Herb Dressing, 79
  Tzatziki, 79
  Yoghurt Dressing, 58
Dundee Cake, 180
E
Edward's Apple and Rhubarb
  Crumble Cake, 142
Edward's Chocolate Éclairs, 32
Edward's Christmas Canapés, 170-174
Edward's Multiseed Brown Bread, 17
Edward's Special Raspberry
  Meringue Cake, 165
Edward's Tortilla Espanola with
  Chorizo, 18
Eggs Benedict, 15
F
Festive Mince Pie Crumbles, 187
Figs: Salad of Roasted Figs, Gorgonzola
Cheese and Parma Ham, 107
Fillet of Beef, Spinach, Mushroom and
Shallots with Black Pepper Cream Sauce,
133
Fish
  Baked Lemon Sole with Salsa Verde,
  137
  Crock of Mussels in a White Wine and
  Cream Broth, 128
  Crusted Hake with Crunchy Pine Nut
  Topping, 130
  Fish Stock, 100
  Pan-Seared Scallops, Lemon and
  Sundried Tomato Butter, 170
  Penne Pasta Salad with Poached
  Salmon, Roasted Fennel and Lemon
  Mayonnaise, 71
  Seafood Vol-au-Vents, 173
  Smoked Haddock Chowder, 100
  Spaghetti with Crab Meat and Chilli,
  129
  Spaghetti with Sweet Chilli Prawns, 87
  Tandoori Salmon, Spicy Mango and
  Cucumber Salsa, 109
  Thai-style Crab Cocktail on Mini
  Wholemeal Scones, 174
  Whole Roasted Sea Bass Stuffed with
  Lemongrass Chilli, 63
Fish, Stock, 100
G
Garlic
  Garlic and Herb Butter, 103
  Garlic and Rosemary Scented Steaks,
  57
  Garlic and Rosemary Smeared Lamb

Cutlets with Garlic Sautéed Potatoes,
  Garlic Sautéed Potatoes, 103
Glazed Fruit Tart, 40
Gluten Free Baking: Lemon and
  Almond Cake, 27
Gorgonzola Cheese: Salad of Roasted
  Figs, Gorganzola Cheese and Parma
  Ham, 107
Gravy, Cranberry, 176
Gravy, Traditional, 155
Guacamole with Home-Baked Spiced
  Tortilla Chips, 106
H
Hake: Crusty Hake with Crunchy Pine
Nut Topping, 130
Hollandaise Sauce, 15
Hot and Spicy Beef Curry, 158
Hungarian Beef Goulash, 85
I
Iced Cupcakes, 28
Italian Baked Chicken, 95
K
Kedgeree, 14
L
Lamb Chops
  Garlic and Rosemary Smeared Lamb
  Cutlets with Garlic Sautéed Potatoes,
  Garlic and Herb Butter, 103
  Mixed Grill Skewers, 13
Lamb, Mince
  Spiced Lamb Koftas with Yoghurt
  Dressing, 58
Lamb, Stewing: Rich Lamb Casserole
with Gratin Topping, 161
Leek
  Creamy Potato, Leek and Thyme
  Soup, 127
  Crispy Beef Spring Rolls, 115
  Spiced Chickpea Broth, 96
  Spiced Winter Vegetable Soup, 148
Lemon
  Baked Lemon Sole with Salsa Verde,
  137
  Crusted Hake with Crunchy Pine Nut
  Toppping, 130
  Lemon and Almond Cake, 27
  Lemon and Ginger Fish Parcels, 54
  Lemon Drizzle Slices, 39
  New Style Coronation Chicken, 154
  Pan-Seared Scallops, Lemon and
  Sundried Tomato Butter, 170
  Penne Pasta Salad with Poached
  Salmon, Roasted Fennel and Lemon
  Mayonnaise, 71
  Whole Roasted Chicken, Lemon, Cour-
  gette and Pine Nut Stuffing, 92
Lemon and Almond Cake, 27
Lemon and Sundried Tomato Butter, 170
Lemon, Courgette & Pine Nut Stuffing, 92
Lemon Drizzle Slices, 39
Lemon Mayonnaise, 71
Lemon Sole, Baked with Salsa Verde, 137
Lemon Syrup, 27
Lemongrass
  Whole Roasted Sea Bass Stuffed with

Lemongrass Chilli, 63
Little Pots of Paté, 152
M
Mango: Tandoori Salmon, Spicy Mango
and Cucumber Salsa, 109
Mediterranean Vegetable Stack, 149
Meringue, 165
Mini Bruschetta with Red Onion
  Marmalade and Blue Cheese, 170
Mini Wholemeal Scones, 174
Mixed Grill Skewers, 13
Monkfish: Seafood Skewers, 60
Moroccan Couscous, 72
Muffuletta, 21
Mushrooms
  Fillet of Beef with Sautéed Spinach and
  Mushroom with Black Pepper Sauce,
  133
  Mediterranean Vegetable Stack, 149
Mushrooms, Wild
  Beef Stroganoff, 108
  Spaghetti with Sweet Chilli Prawns, 87
Mussels, Crock of in a White Wine and
  Cream Broth, 128
Mustard Seed Dressing, 79
N
New Style Coronation Chicken, 154
Noodles
  Beef and Vegetable Noodle Stir Fry,
  88
  Sweet Chilli Noodle Salad, 68
O
Orange and Cinnamon Glaze, 24
P
Pan-Seared Scallops, Lemon and
  Sundried Tomato Butter, 170
Parma Ham
  Muffuletta, 21
  Salad of Roasted Figs, Gorgonzola
  and Parma Ham, 107
Pastry, Biscuit, 40
Pastry, Choux, 32
Pastry Cream, 40
Pastry, Sweet, 187
Pastry, Short Crust, 121
Pear: Baked Ginger Pudding, Cinnamon
Roasted Pears with Butterscotch Sauce,
138
Penne Pasta Salad with Poached Salmon,
  Roasted Fennel and Lemon
  Mayonnaise, 71
Penne Pasta with Chunky Sausages and
  Tomato Cream Sauce, 49
Pesto and Sundried Tomato Bread, 146
Pine Nuts
  Crusted Hake with Crunchy Pine Nut
  Topping, 130
  Potato Salad with Pesto, Pine Nuts and
  Smoked Bacon, 75
  Whole Roasted Chicken, Lemon, Cour-
  gette and Pine Nut Stuffing, 92
Potatoes
  Creamy Potato, Leek and Thyme
  Soup, 127
  Crisper than Crisp Potato Wedges, 117

Edward's Tortilla Espanola with Chorizo, 18
Garlic Sautéd Potatoes, 103
Potato Salad with Pesto Pine Nuts and Smoked Bacon, 75
Rich Lamb Casserole with Gratin Topping, 161
Pork and Chicken Terrine, 151
Pork and Cider Stroganoff, 90
Pork Salad, Crispy, with Cashew Nuts and
Sweet Potato Crisps, 82
Pork, Minced
Pork and Chicken Terrine, 151
Pork Steak
Pork and Cider Stroganoff, 90
Pork Steak Stuffed with Curried Rice, 134
Potato Salad with Pesto Pine Nuts and Smoked Bacon, 75
Prawns
Seafood Skewers, 60
Spaghetti with Sweet Chilli Prawns, 87
Pudding
Baked Ginger Pudding, Cinnamon Roasted Pears with Butterscotch Sauce, 138
Steamed Chocolate Pudding, Chocolate and Baileys Sauce, 162
Q
Quiche in a Tin, 121
R
Raspberries
Edward's Special Raspberry Meringue Cake, 165
White Chocolate and Raspberry Trifle, 183
Red Onion Marmalade, 170
Mini Bruschetta with Red Onion Marmalade and Blue Cheese, 170
Muffuletta, 21
Rhubarb: Edward's Apple and Rhubarb Crumble Cake, 142
Rich Lamb Casserole with Gratin Topping, 161
Roast Sirloin Beef, Traditional Gravy, 155
Roasted Carrot and Ginger Soup, 99
Rocket
Mini Bruschetta with Red Onion Marmalade and Blue Cheese, 170
Muffuletta, 21
Thai-Style Crab Cocktail on Mini Wholemeal Scones, 174
Rosemary
Delicious Dressings, 79
Garlic and Rosemary Scented Steaks, 57
Garlic and Rosemary Smeared Lamb Cutlets with Garlic Sautéd Potatoes, Garlic and Herb Butter, 103
Mixed Grill Skewers, 13
Rosemary and Balsamic Infusion, 79
S
Salad
Crispy Pork Salad with Cashew Nuts

and Sweet Potato Crisps, 82
Penne Pasta Salad with Poached Salmon, Roasted Fennel and Lemon Mayonnaise, 71
Potato Salad with Pesto Pine Nuts and Smoked Bacon, 75
Salad of Roasted Figs, Gorgonzola Cheese and Parma Ham, 107
Salad of Roasted Figs, Gorgonzola Cheese and Parma Ham, 107
Salad Selections, 76
Sweet Chilli Noodle Salad, 68
Salad of Roasted Figs, Gorgonzola Cheese and Parma Ham, 107
Salmon
Asian Crusted Salmon, 157
Lemon and Ginger Fish Parcels, 54
Penne Pasta Salad with Poached Salmon, Roasted Fennel and Lemon Mayonnaise, 71
Seafood Skewers, 60
Seafood Vol-au-Vents, 173
Tandoori Salmon, Spicy Mango and Cucumber Salsa, 109
Salsa Verde, 137
Scallops
Pan-Seared Scallops, Lemon and Sundried Tomato Butter, 170
Seafood Skewers, 60
Sea Bass
Whole Roasted Sea Bass Stuffed with Lemongrass Chilli, 63
Seafood Skewers, 60
Seafood Vol-au-Vents, 173
Sesame Chicken Goujons, 47
Smoked Haddock
Kedgeree, 14,
Smoked Haddock Chowder, 100
Smoked Haddock Chowder, 100
Spaghetti with Crab Meat and Chilli, 129
Spaghetti with Sweet Chilli Prawns, 87
Spaghetti Bolognaise, 48
Spiced Chickpea Broth, 96
Spiced Hot Cross Buns with Orange Cinnamon Glaze, 24
Spiced Indian Pakoras, 84
Spiced Lamb Koftas with Yoghurt Dressing, 58
Spiced Winter Vegetable Soup, 148
Spicy Chicken Quesadillas, 114
Spicy Mango and Cucumber Salsa, 109
Spinach
Fillet of Beef with Sautéd Spinach and Mushroom with Black Pepper Cream Sauce, 133
Spiced Indian Pakoras, 84
Sponge, 51
Steamed Chocolate Pudding, Chocolate and Baileys Sauce, 162
Sugar-Crusted Cherry Scones, 35
Summer Herb Dressing, 79
Sundried Tomato
Pan-Seared Scallops, Lemon and Sundried Tomato Butter, 170

Pesto and Sundried Tomato Bread, 146
Thai-Style Crab Cocktail on Mini Wholemeal Scones, 174
Sweet and Sticky Chicken Drumsticks, 44
Sweet Chilli Jam
Spaghetti with Sweet Chilli Prawns, 87
Sweet Chilli Noodle Salad, 68
Sweet Chilli Noodle Salad, 68
Sweet Chilli Sauce
Beef and Vegetable Noodle Stir Fry, 88
Spicy Chicken Quesdillas, 114
Thai-Style Crab Cocktail with Mini Wholemeal Scones, 174
Sweet Potatoes
Crispy Pork Salad with Cashew Nuts and Sweet Potato Crisps, 82
Spiced Winter Vegetable Soup, 148
Sweet Potato Crisps, 82
Swiss Roll, 183
T
Tandoori Salmon, Spicy Mango and Cucumber Salsa, 109
Thai-Style Crab Cocktail on Mini Wholemeal Scones, 174
Tortilla Crisps, 106
Tortilla Wrap
Mediterranean Vegetable Stack, 149
Spicy Chicken Quesadillas, 114
Traditional Mincemeat, 184
Traditional Roast Turkey Breast with Cranberry Gravy, 176
Tzatziki, 79
V
Vanilla
Chocolate Chip Cookies, 36
Glazed Fruit Tart, 40
Iced Cupcakes, 28
Vegetarian Moussaka, 179
W
Walnuts
Apple and Walnut Stuffing, 177
Moroccan Couscous, 72
White Chocolate and Raspberry Trifle, 183
White Chocolate Custard, 183
White Soda Scones with Cheese and Thyme, 124
Whole Roast Duck with Apricot and Hazelnut Stuffing, 178
Whole Roasted Chicken, Lemon, Courgettes and Pine Nut Stuffing, 92
Whole Roasted Sea Bass Stuffed with Lemongrass Chilli, 63
Y
Yoghurt Dressing, 58